WITHDR

A CONFLICT
OF INTEREST

A CONFLICT OF INTEREST

Women in German Social Democracy, 1919–1933

Renate Pore

Contributions in Women's Studies, Number 26

GREENWOOD PRESS
Westport, Connecticut • London, England

Library of Congress Cataloging in Publication Data

Pore, Renate.
  A conflict of interest.

  (Contributions in women's studies ; no. 26 ISSN 0147-104X)
  Bibliography: p.
  Includes index.
  1. Feminism—Germany—History. 2. Women's rights—
Germany—History. 3. Sozialdemokratische Partei
Deutschlands. 4. Women in politics—Germany—History.
5. Germany—History—1918-1933. I. Title.
II. Series.
HQ1627.P73   305.4'2'0943   80-27183
ISBN 0-313-22856-6 (lib. bdg.)

Library of Congress Catalog Card Number: 80-27183
ISBN: 0-313-22856-6
ISSN: 0147-104X

First published in 1981

Greenwood Press
A division of Congressional Information Service, Inc.
88 Post Road West, Westport, Connecticut 06881

Printed in the United States of America

10 9 8 7 6 5 4 3 2 1

To the memory of my grandmother,
Margarete Marx, 1904–1978

CONTENTS

PREFACE

THIS STUDY ENDEAVORS to promote an understanding of the contradictions faced by a movement for women's liberation that was to some extent separate but still a part of a larger movement for social change. It seeks to understand how those contradictions were reconciled and to what extent being a part of a larger movement was advantageous to the liberation of women and to what extent it was not.

It is indicative of the politics of scholarship that the issues raised in this study have contemporary relevance and were first raised in the midst of a new women's movement in 1975. Juliet Mitchell has called the struggle for women's liberation "the longest revolution," and it is with an alternating sense of exhiliration and dismay that one reads about the struggles, issues, and debates of the 1890s and the 1920s and hears them in the struggles, issues, and debates of today. It is exhilarating to discover the historical roots of the women's movement; it is discouraging to understand that the dimensions of the struggle have not changed significantly and that the feminist consciousness of one generation is not passed automatically to the next but can disappear for a generation or more before bursting forth anew. It was with mixed emotions that I participated in a day-long meeting of Social Democratic women in Bonn-Bad Godesberg in 1975 and heard them raise the same issues that had preoccupied their grandmothers and great-grandmothers; and it is with similar emotions that I experience the continuing conflict between socialism and feminism, which, despite some good attempts at synthesis, continues to mark the theory and practice of the left, from democratic socialists to Marxist-Leninists.

As a feminist activist, I find that the conflicts raised by German Social Democratic women in the 1920s have become personally familiar; and although this book sometimes assumes a critical tone, I do not wish to suggest that I have anything but the greatest admiration for the women who are the focus of this study.

I am indebted to the Fulbright Commission and its generous program for making possible the research for this study in Germany. A year away from home and Christy would have been more difficult without the affection of my family in Treis—Omi, Adolf, and Irmgard Marx—and the many kind people in Bonn, particularly my friends John and Maria Tagliabue, Suzanne and Cliff Toliver, Woon-Hong Lee, Hans-Joachim Kunz, and Frau Liselotte Franzky.

I will always be grateful to John A. Maxwell for nurturing the scholar and the feminist in me and for being the first to suggest that the two were not mutually exclusive. Without the special encouragement of Susie Ross, Betty Justice, and Steve Legeay, this publication would not have been possible.

INTRODUCTION

DURING THE COURSE of the nineteenth century, almost everywhere in the industrializing nations of the West, organized women's movements emerged to protest and change the existing status of women in society and personal life. Because women experienced oppression in a wide variety of ways, depending upon their nationality, race, social class, and, not insignificantly, the nature of their relationships with the men in their lives—fathers, lovers, mentors, and husbands—no unifying ideology or common strategy was developed to direct the desired change. All worked for the liberation of women, but there was little agreement on what liberation meant or how it should best be pursued. This was true in the United States, where that part of the organized women's movement that eventually focused on the vote found the radical feminism of the pioneers of the American women's movement unsavory and detrimental to their aims.[1] It was also true in Germany, where those seeking to improve the status of women had different agendas and were sometimes in hostile opposition to one another.

By the 1890s, there were two distinct women's movements in Germany, one socialist, the other liberal middle class, or bourgeois (*bürgerlich*). Both of these movements had further divisions within them. Those groups characterized as bourgeois and organized into the Union of German Women's Organizations (Bund Deutscher Frauenvereine, or BDF) by 1894 ranged from radical

feminists who believed that the liberation of women would re-
quire economic, social, and political change as well as a change
in sexual relationships, to those who were content to focus on
providing more educational or professional opportunities for
women and those who insisted that they wanted rights not for
themselves but to promote the general welfare.[2] What distinguished all of the tendencies of the bourgeois women's movement from the socialist was not so much a difference in issues,
for the radical branch of the bourgeois women's movement
shared many of the concerns of the socialists, including a concern for the particular oppression of working-class women. It
was rather the socialist women's identification as women and
as members of the working class, and their ties to an organized
mass political party, the German Social Democratic Party (SPD).

The SPD had come into existence in 1875 through the merger
of two socialist parties, Ferdinand Lassalle's General German
Workers' Association and Wilhelm Liebknecht and August Bebel's
Social Democratic Labor Party. Lassalleans hoped for socialism
to be achieved through the introduction of democracy. Liebknecht and Bebel were disciples of Marx and believers in revolutionary socialism. The twin heritage of Lassallean socialism and
Marxian socialism provided the basis for the Social Democrats'
program, divided into long-run objectives and immediate aims
to be realized within capitalist society.[3] This dual emphasis was
very much reflected in the strategy of the socialist women's
movement.

German socialism expanded after 1875 in response to the industrialization of Germany and the growth of an industrial
proletariat, which made up almost 40 percent of the work force
by 1900. As a political party, the SPD represented the new working class in the German parliament, but the inequities of the German political system assured that the party would never wield
any real power or influence through the existing system. The
significance of German Social Democracy in the nineteenth
century, however, went beyond the limited function as a political
party. For the new urban working class, it provided a way of life,
a subculture that promoted new values and permitted questioning not only of traditional economic relationships but of polit-

ical, social, and personal ones as well. Thus it provided a fertile
ground for the growth of a women's movement within the con-
text of a socialist movement.[4]

From the Utopians of the nineteenth century to Marx and
Engels, socialist theoreticians had always supported the liberation of women; and the leading figure in German Social Democracy, August Bebel, continued this tradition in his popular
book, *Woman under Socialism.* Of course, not all members
of the working class or the SPD supported women's liberation,
as was evident in intense debates within the party. Nevertheless,
in 1891, the SPD officially endorsed and supported the emancipation of women. In that year, the party became the first major
political party to make the vote and political equality part of its
programmatic demands.

More significant, however, was the party's support for the organization of a socialist women's movement under the leadership of Clara Zetkin. Until World War I, this women's movement
understood the emancipation of women in doctrinaire revolutionary Marxist terms, stressing that the "woman question" was iden-
tical with the "social question" and that women's liberation
would coincide with the liberation of the working class and the
advent of socialism. In the meantime, the task for a women's
movement was to bring the docile, family-centered woman up
to the political level of men to make her a better soldier in the
coming class struggle. In this task, Zetkin sometimes ran into
conflict with socialist comrades, whom she attacked as back-
ward and as no better than the most bourgeois Philistines in
their attitudes toward women.[5]

Zetkin battled within the Social Democratic movement for
acceptance for women's liberation and for autonomy for the
women's movement; nevertheless, she always identified primarily as a revolutionary socialist and disdained making any
alliance with bourgeois women, even when they fought for the
same issues. Those pre-World War I socialist women who felt
an affinity with the more progressive elements of the bourgeois
women's movement never successfully challenged this focus.
The way Zetkin defined it, there was no conflict of interest between being a socialist and the struggle for women's emancipa-

tion. Equality was a critical, but only first, step in the struggle for socialism. That is not to say that Zetkin and her followers were not also feminists in our understanding of the term. They were feminists insofar as they identified as women and understood that as women they had special interests to promote and protect and that sometimes this required struggling with men of their own class. They also adopted what Jean Quataert has described as feminist tactics, that is, they insisted on maintaining a separate organization, separate meetings, and a journal addressed to women.[6] The creation of a separate women's movement was initially necessitated by the repressive laws of Wilhelminian Germany, which made political activity by women illegal; but after 1908, when those laws were repealed, the women's movement still maintained its autonomy.

Of course, there was never any question that the liberation of women necessitated the restructuring of society and that this required the cooperation of all of those who were oppressed under capitalism—men as well as women. Working-class men and women might struggle with each other, but ultimately their interests were the same. This meant that when unity was perceived as critical, women's interests were submerged for the interests of the socialist movement.[7] Before World War I, when the power of the SPD was more potential than real, when the party's tactics were those of pure opposition and parliament was used primarily as a platform for agitation, the women's movement was not particularly limited by this conflict. Criticisms leveled at the women's movement reflected the divisions between left and moderate socialists more than between men and women.

World War I and the events that followed changed the political reality of the SPD and the women's movement. The crisis of war triggered a long-developing schism, as the left wing, including Clara Zetkin, left the majority party. Imperial Germany collapsed, and in 1919 a new democratic republic was born in which the SPD was to be a powerful political force. In the 1920s, the SPD changed its emphasis from agitation and opposition to winning votes and reforming German society through the institutions of parliamentary democracy. Changes for the SPD brought

significant changes for the socialist women's movement as well.
Most significant was a new leadership, handpicked by Friedrich
Ebert and approved by the moderate wing of the party. Under
the direction of Marie Juchacz, the new women's movement
promised to heed the interests of the party and to respond to
its direction. Reform, not revolution, was to be its strategy.

A new democratic constitution and the granting of suffrage
in 1919 made working within the system possible for women
for the first time in German history. They were elated, and
Marie Juchacz proclaimed German women to be the freest in
the world. No one believed that the vote and constitutional
equality had liberated women in Germany, but they did believe
that the foundations for real progress had been laid. In this
they shared the belief of women everywhere who, after decades
of hard work, suddenly found themselves enfranchised.

Like social feminists in the United States, who "submerged
their interests as women in a sea of worthy enterprises,"[8] and
bourgeois feminists in Germany, Social Democratic women in
the 1920s decided that new rights meant new duties and identified and then carved out social welfare work as a prime area
of focus. In this they were praised by the men of their party
for doing that work in society for which women were best
suited. Just as the entrance of women into the industrial labor
force had resulted in distinct male and female divisions of labor,
so the entrance of women into political life created separate
spheres of interest for men and women. For Social Democratic
women, and women everywhere, the emphasis on social welfare
work presented a conflict of interest to their goal of emancipation. It sapped energy and members from the political work,
and it reinforced traditional views of women, which Social
Democratic women were attempting to overcome.

While many Social Democratic women delivered social
welfare services, some became politicians in parliament, where
they focused on social welfare issues. More women were members of parliament in Germany in the 1920s than in the United
States or most other Western countries, but the Weimar system
assured that women delegates rarely, if ever, acted independently.
Thus the new democratic system did not provide a vehicle for

the independent action of women, socialist or bourgeois. Parliament was not the body where Social Democratic women could
realize their goals except insofar as those goals were in accord
with the party. With perhaps one important exception, the goals
of the SPD and the goals of Social Democratic women appeared
not to be in conflict in parliament. The SPD sponsored much
progressive legislation in the interests of women, including divorce and abortion reform, and toward the end of the decade
it consistently supported the right of women to work for wages.
Within parliament, the SPD must have appeared to be the best
allies women could have. Most of the progressive legislation to
benefit women was sponsored by the SPD; and if its effect was
not great, it was due more to the limitations of the parliamentary
system, which required compromises, than to the intent of the
SPD.

Within the party, many of the same issues that had characterized the relationship between men and women before the war
continued. Women insisted that, as they were still disadvantaged,
their separate organizations, meetings, and journals should continue to exist. On this issue they won. When they suggested,
however, that women should meet before rather than after the
general party congress, they were lectured that it was the function of the women's meetings to understand the interests of the
party and to work out strategies for promoting those interests
among women. Women continued to complain about male attitudes, charging, as Clara Zetkin had, that the proletariat male
differed little from his bourgeois counterpart in his concept of
women as property. Thus women had to contend with the conflict of working within a party where personally most men were
attached to traditional relations between the sexes and a party
that supported a women's movement but which in the 1920s
viewed that movement strategically as a vehicle for gaining members and voters for the SPD.

Finally, there was the conflict created by the uncritical ad-
herence to the old socialist theory of women's emancipation,
which provided only limited guidance for women's liberation
in the 1920s. It helped Social Democratic women understand
that political equality was not particularly meaningful without

economic equality. It put the emphasis on remunerative work for women and social welfare legislation to ease the burden of the working-class woman and mother, but it did not lead to an analysis of the way women continued to experience oppression. It did not lead to an understanding of the division of labor, nor to the meaning of clerical and other white-collar jobs opening to women, nor to an understanding of the contradictions between men and women in sexual relationships and the family. As individuals, Social Democratic women struggled with the latter issue in the 1920s, but there was no organized attack.

Despite the conflicts women faced in representing their interests within the party, despite the conflicts engendered by a political system that required a compromise of principles for short-range political goals, the SPD probably provided the best opportunity for women's interests to be represented in the new democratic WeimarRepublic. After World War II, Marie Juchacz said that the Social Democratic Women's Movement had not had enough time to do its work.[9] She believed that progress was being made when the movement was destroyed in 1933 by German fascism. We cannot know whether or not the conflicts faced by Social Democratic women in the 1920s would have eventually been resolved in favor of women's liberation; we can only conclude that working within a progressive political party is fraught with both opportunities and dangers for women's liberation.

NOTES

1. See, for example, Aileen S. Kraditor, *The Ideas of the Women's Suffrage Movement, 1890-1920* (Garden City, New York, 1971), p. 7.

2. For studies on the bourgeois women's movement in Germany, see Richard J. Evans, *The Feminist Movement in Germany, 1894-1933* (London, 1976), and Amy Hackett, "The Politics of Feminism in Wilhelmine Germany, 1890-1918" (Ph.D. dissertation, Columbia University, 1976).

3. Carl E. Schorske, *German Social Democracy, 1905-1917: The Development of the Great Schism* (New York, 1972), pp. 1-27.

4. Jean H. Quataert, *Reluctant Feminists in German Social Democracy, 1885-1917* (Princeton, New Jersey, 1979), pp. 3-17.

5. At the SPD Women's Conference in 1900, Zetkin said, "In theory the women comrades are already equal; in practice, however, the male

comrades are as Philistine as any bourgeois." Zetkin's colorful expression does not translate well. The German reads: "In der Theorie sind die Genossinen schon gleichberechtigt, in der Praxis aber hängt der Philisterzopf den männlichen Genossen noch ebenso im Nacken wie dem ersten besten Spiessbürger." Quoted in Marie Juchacz, *Sie lebten für eine bessere Welt* (Berlin, 1955), p. 68. All translations from the German in this study are the author's.

    6. Quataert, *Reluctant Feminists*, p. 13.

    7. Quataert cites birth control as such an issue. Jean H. Quataert, "Unequal Partners in an Uneasy Alliance: Women and the Working Class in Imperial Germany," in Jean H. Quataert and Marilyn J. Boxer, eds., *Socialist Women: European Socialist Feminism in the Nineteenth and Early Twentieth Centuries* (New York, 1978), pp. 127-128.

    8. William L. O'Neill, "Feminism as a Radical Ideology," in Alfred F. Young, ed., *Dissent: Explorations in the History of American Radicalism* (De Kalb, Illinois, 1968), p. 283. For further discussion on social feminism in the United States, see also J. Stanley Lemons, *The Woman Citizen: Social Feminism in the 1920s* (Urbana, Illinois, 1975).

    9. Juchacz, *Sie lebten für eine bessere Welt*, p. 11.

A CONFLICT OF INTEREST

1

THE SOCIAL DEMOCRATIC WOMEN'S MOVEMENT IN THEORY AND PRACTICE, 1890-1914

OUT OF THE intellectual and social ferment of the eighteenth century, socialism and feminism emerged as ideologies promising the liberation of the individual from oppressive social conditions. The progress of industrialization, which changed social relationships and family life, provided the stimulus for the advance of both of these ideologies into full-fledged organized international movements by the latter half of the nineteenth century.[1]

Feminism, in its bourgeois expression, was the natural extension of eighteenth-century liberalism, extending the natural rights of man to woman. It was primarily middle class, with the liberal individualistic belief that the emancipation of women depended upon the removal of legal restraints that inhibited women's ability to act as free individuals. The classic program of the bourgeois feminists emphasized middle-class rights: the right to vote, the right to control property and earnings within marriage, the right to education and entrance into the professions. Feminism generally did not make a connection between the oppression of women and other social classes. Socialism, on the other hand, did make such a connection.

From their earliest theorists, socialists had incorporated the emancipation of women into their model of an egalitarian society. Nineteenth-century Marxist socialists, while emphasizing the class nature of society and the oppression of the working class under capitalism, continued this tradition. All of the socialist theoreticians, from the Utopian socialists to Marx, Engels, and Bebel, had a clear commitment to the emancipation of women and recognized that women experienced a double oppression as women and as members of the working class.

THE SOCIALIST THEORY OF WOMEN'S EMANCIPATION

In general, socialist theory advanced the view that the basis of women's oppression was economic. Women's subordinate position within the family and society was based on the economic power of the father/husband, and the key to liberation was the achievement of economic independence. In order to gain economic independence, the theory proposed, women would have to leave the home and engage in socially productive work. In capitalist society, however, this could not bring real liberation, since women would merely be exchanging one kind of dependence in the home for another kind in the factory. As socially productive workers, women would find themselves in the same position as men of the working class, whose liberation could come only when work was liberated from capital. When capitalist production was replaced by socialism, the theory suggested, women would be both socially productive and liberated and would take their rightful place in society as the equals of men.

The eighteenth-century Utopian socialists believed that the institution of the patriarchal family and the existing relationship between the sexes presented one of the major hindrances to the creation of a harmonious, unrepressive society. A sexually liberated society, where women were freed from the domination of men, was central to the Utopian vision. For Charles Fourier, one of the foremost Utopian socialists, the degree of emancipation of women was a measure of the general advance of civilization:

The change in an historical epoch can always be determined by the progress of woman toward freedom, because in the relation of woman to man, of the weak to the strong, the victory of human nature over brutality is most evident. The degree of feminine emancipation is the natural measure of general emancipation.[2]

Although the Utopian socialists had many curious and interesting ideas about the status of women and how to change the existing relationship between the sexes, perhaps their greatest significance lay in their application of the principle of exploitation to both worker and woman, a concept subsequently taken over by Marx and his heirs.

Neither Marx nor Engels ever produced a comprehensive or definitive work on the woman question, but both were keenly aware of the sexual inequality in bourgeois society; and references to the "woman question" can be found throughout their published writings and private correspondence.[3] "The general condition of women in modern society is an inhuman one," they observed in *The Holy Family*, but more significant than such comments on the condition of women was their analysis of capitalist society, which provided a theory of the cause of women's oppression that would be elaborated on by later socialist thinkers such as August Bebel and Clara Zetkin[4] and would provide the theoretical basis for an organized movement.

In the *Communist Manifesto* (1848), their call to action and their classic analysis of capitalist society, Marx and Engels established the basis for the Marxist critique of the oppression of women under capitalism. They agreed with the Utopian socialists that the patriarchal family was the institutional source of the oppression and exploitation of women. Based on exploitative economic relationships, the patriarchal family, they charged, perverted the most intimate and potentially rewarding human relationship. In capitalist society, women in their procreative function were exploited as instruments of production. Despite bourgeois attempts to mystify the family and to cloak it in love and sentiment, the bourgeois patriarchal family was an institution based on economic interests, on private gain, and was inherently exploitative and oppressive.[5]

Many years after the *Manifesto*, Engels again took up this theme in *The Origin of the Family, Private Property, and the State*. Published in 1884, *Origin of the Family* was based on the research of the controversial nineteenth-century American anthropologist Lewis H. Morgan and attempted to explain how the oppression of women coincided with changing economic relationships and consequent changes in the family, private property, and the state.

Origin of the Family theorized that prehistoric, precivilized society, which made up the greater part of human history, was characterized by collective ownership of property and group marriage. While there was a division of labor, with men hunting and women attending to affairs around the community, there was no surplus, and thus no group or individual in these societies could gain an advantage over another. Children belonged to their mothers, and paternity was unknown and irrelevant. As a result of their procreative function, women enjoyed a high and respected position, and a state of equality existed between the sexes.

Gradually, new economic developments, such as the domestication of animals and the breeding of herds, developed new sources of wealth controlled by men, resulting in a change in the existing equal and harmonious social relationships. The new economic relationship eventually expressed itself in social relationships by a change in the existing group marriage to a pairing marriage, where one man lived with one woman. The pairing marriage was distinguished from the later monogamous marriage in that it was not oppressive to women. Women continued to exert a great deal of control within the marriage, the children continued to belong to them, and the marriage could easily be dissolved. The change from group to pairing marriage, Engels speculated, was instigated by and in the best interests of women, for as population grew and the material conditions of life changed, sexual relationships with many men, Engels believed, must have become increasingly oppressive to women, and therefore they opted for a more permanent relationship with one man.[6]

As new wealth in the form of herds passed into the private possession of families and multiplied, it struck a blow at society founded on pairing marriage and mother-right. While the new wealth was controlled by the man, the children belonged to the woman. This became increasingly undesirable to men, who wanted to assure that their property was passed to their biologic children. To ensure biologic paternity, men forced women into monogamous marriage. With the advent of monogamy, descent was reckoned no longer through the female but through the male. This, Engels wrote, was the world-historic defeat of the female sex, one of the most decisive revolutions in history.[7] How and when this revolution took place Engels did not pretend to know, but he insisted that there was extensive proof for the existence of mother-right before father-right. For this evidence, Engels relied not only on the research of Lewis H. Morgan but also on the work of the nineteenth-century classical scholar John Jacob Bachofen.[8]

Subsequent legal, social, political, and religious developments all reflected the defeat of mother-right, assuring the continuing dominance of the male. Monogamy, Engels wrote, which was an advance for civilization and which under different circumstances might have been the highest form of relationship between the sexes, thus appeared as the subjection of one sex by the other and the proclamation of the conflict between the sexes.

> The first division of labour is that between man and woman for child breeding. . . . The first class antagonism which appears in history coincides with the development of the antagonism between man and woman in monogamian marriage, and the first class oppression with that of the female sex by the male. Monogamy was a great historical advance, but at the same time it inaugurated, along with slavery and private wealth, that epoch lasting until today, in which the well-being and development of the one group are attained by the misery and repression of the other.[9]

Twentieth-century theorists have some disagreement with Engels' account of the defeat of the female sex by the male having its origin in the economic organization of society. Simone de Beauvoir, in *The Second Sex*, as well as more recent feminist theorists, such as Juliet Mitchell and Shulamith Firestone, all have focused on the inadequacy of explaining the oppression of women solely from a Marxist historical materialist perspective.[10]

De Beauvoir proposed that the sexual imbalance of power was originally not economically but biologically determined. There never was a reciprocal or equal relation between the sexes, according to de Beauvoir. Woman was always perceived by man as different, as "the Other," from the moment that man became aware of himself.

Thus the triumph of the patriarchate was neither a matter of chance nor the result of violent revolution. From humanity's beginnings, their biological advantage has enabled the males to affirm their status as sole and sovereign subjects; they have never abdicated this position; they once relinquished a part of their independent existence to Nature and to Woman; but afterward they won it back. Condemned to play the part of the Other, woman was also condemned to hold only uncertain power: slave or idol, it was never she who chose her lot.[11]

While de Beauvoir disagreed with Engels on the original cause of woman's subjection, she agreed that her continued oppression was tied to existing economic relationships.[12]

Another serious criticism of Engels comes from modern social anthropologists, many of whom have rejected Morgan's thesis of a universal evolutionary development from matriarchal to patriarchal society. If there was no prehistoric matriarchy, then Engels' proposition that men established their domination over women when they came to control property loses credibility.[13]

Whatever its biases and scholarly defects, *Origin of the Family* has succeeded perfectly as a scathing polemic on the nineteenth-century bourgeois family. Whether the development from matriarchy to patriarchy was a universal development was not as significant as stripping away the nineteenth-century sentiment and illusion surrounding the family and revealing its essentially economic nature. Publicizing the existence of other forms of marriage and social relationships, and theories of how contemporary forms of family life evolved or might have evolved, also helped dispel some of the myths of "woman's nature" that in the nineteenth century was increasingly being used to justify women's inferior status in the family and society.

Marriage among the bourgeoisie, Engels charged, was purely a matter of economics and convenience. The woman in bourgeois marriage differed from the courtesan only "in that she does not let out her body on piecework as a wage-worker, but sells it once and for all into slavery."[14] Women had little choice in this matter, for as long as they continued to work only in private industry (i.e., the home), they were at the mercy of men. The inferior position of the woman in the bourgeois patriarchal family was simply the consequence of her dependence and the male's economic supremacy. With the abolition of the latter, Engels implied, the social, political, and psychological supremacy of men would disappear of itself. "The first premise for the emancipation of women is the reintroduction of the entire female sex into public industry," he offered as his solution to the liberation of women.[15]

The oppression of women as having its base in economic relationships is also the major theme in the best-known socialist work on women, August Bebel's *Woman under Socialism.* August Bebel, the leading and most respected figure in the German Social Democratic movement, had long been concerned with the equality of women. In 1879, shortly after Bismarck's antisocialist laws went into effect in Germany, he published *Woman under Socialism.* Written rather hastily while Bebel was in jail, *Woman under Socialism* went through 50 editions and was translated into every major European language before his death in 1913.[16]

While *Woman under Socialism* was significant for all socialists for presenting the essential ideas of Social Democracy in a popularized, available form, it was especially meaningful for socialist women in Germany. For some, it was the major influence that turned them into activists. The leaders of the women's movement, such as Clara Zetkin and Marie Juchacz, as well as the most brilliant Marxist theoretician of the day, Rosa Luxemburg, all attested to the influence of Bebel's book upon their lives.[17]

In *Woman under Socialism*, Bebel stressed the connection between the social question and the woman question. "Woman and the workingman have since old had this in common—oppression. . . . *There can be no emancipation of humanity without the social independence and equality of the sexes,*" he stated in his introduction.[18] As a revolutionary socialist, Bebel insisted that changing the laws and institutions of the present social order would not begin to liberate women. Although very much aware of the necessity of changing the socialization and educational experiences of women, Bebel, like Engels, taught that economics was the basis of the inequality between the sexes.

> The goal, accordingly, is not merely the realization of the
> equal rights of women with man within present society,
> as is aimed at by the bourgeois woman emancipationists.
> It lies beyond,—the removal of all impediments that make
> man dependent upon man; and, consequently, one sex upon
> the other. Accordingly, the solution of the Woman Question
> coincides completely with the solution of the Social Question.[19]

Bebel recognized, however, that women had an additional problem. They were oppressed not only by the capitalist but also by men of their own class. Furthermore, Bebel wrote, men of all social classes have an interest in maintaining the prevailing inequality between the sexes. Therefore, women must fight not only for the liberation of the working class but for their own liberation as well. And in the struggle for their liberation, women should expect no help from men: "Men gladly accept such a state of things; they are its beneficiaries. It flatters their pride, their vanity, their interest to play the role of the stronger and the master . . . woman should expect as little help from men as workingmen do from the capitalist class."[20]

Bebel, like Engels, also drew upon history to make his case. Tracing the evolution of family life from prehistoric times, through classical Greece and medieval Europe, Bebel showed that there was nothing "natural" about the nineteenth-century status of women and the nineteenth-century form of the family. Like Engels, he relied upon Morgan and Bachofen as his authorities.

The major part of *Women under Socialism* was devoted to an analysis of the condition of women and family life in the nineteenth century. With a great deal of statistical evidence, he pointed to the decline of marriage and family life in nineteenth-century Europe. The increase in divorce, illegitimate births, and prostitution, as well as venereal disease, Bebel blamed on the contradictions between the sexual nature of men and women and bourgeois family life.

Bebel also went further than most socialists and speculated about what woman's life in the future socialist society would be like. All women, like all men, would be engaged in socially productive work. Women's work in the home would be relieved through new technological inventions and through the socialization of many of the functions usually performed in the home, such as child care and food preparation. In addition, the burden for the care of the aged and the ill would be assumed by society as a whole. Not surprisingly, Bebel did not touch on the question of to what extent men would become involved in traditional women's work; he leaves the impression that when child care and cooking are socialized, it will still be women caring for the children and running the communal kitchens. Bebel is typical as a social thinker in looking toward technology to provide the solutions for hard contradictions. Nowhere does he confront the question of men assuming their share of child care and housework, nor does he suggest attacking the sexual division of labor through which sexual discrimination is perpetuated.

Bebel's conclusion was a highly optimistic and inspiring summary of the position of women in the future socialist society and must have been the passage that motivated many a German woman to become active in the cause of her own liberation and that of the working class:

> The woman of the future society is socially and economically independent; she is no longer subject to even a vestige of dominion and exploitation; she is free, the peer of man, the mistress of her lot. Her education is the same as that of man, with such exceptions as the difference of sex and sexual functions demand. Living under natural conditions, she is able to unfold and exercise her mental powers and faculties. She chooses her occupation in such fields as correspond with her wishes, inclinations and natural abilities, and she works under conditions identical with man's. . . . In the choice of love, she is, like man, free and unhampered. She woos or is wooed, and closes the bond from no considerations other

than her own inclinations. This bond is a private contract,
celebrated without the intervention of any functionary. . . .[21]

The transition from the purely theoretical work of Engels
and Bebel to an activist women's movement was made by Clara
Zetkin. She synthesized and articulated the problem of women
for the socialist parties at the Paris International of 1889, at
which the German Social Democratic Party first committed itself officially to the emancipation of women and gave direction
for an organized Social Democratic Women's Movement in
Germany.

Zetkin's views, which she presented at the Paris International,
were published that same year in a pamphlet entitled *Die
Arbeiterinnen und Frauenfrage der Gegenwart (Working Women
and the Contemporary Woman Question)*. This pamphlet summarized with great theoretical clarity and consistency the major
points of Marx, Engels, and Bebel and provided the direction for
the future political course of the Social Democratic Party in
regard to the theory of women's emancipation.

Zetkin reaffirmed the socialist notion that women had been
oppressed since the overthrow of the prehistoric matriarchy and
that the subjection of women, which had come to seem like an
eternal verity supported by religion and other traditional institutions, was nothing more than the result of a particular economic
organization. With the advent of industrialization came the opportunity to change the economic organization of society and for
the first time the possible liberation of women. Industrialization
forced women from the home into the factory, freeing them from
their economic dependence in the family.

Zetkin's concise articulation of this issue came at a time when
many socialists believed that cheap female labor was one of the
major obstacles to the economic advancement of the working
class and clamored for the exclusion of women from industrial
work.[22] She was an important force in steering the party away
from such a hopelessly unrealistic position, arguing vehemently
that the only way to combat the system that depressed wages
was not to deny work to women but to socialize the means of
production. The liberation of women and men depended upon

the liberation of labor from capital, she reminded socialist men. One of the first steps toward this liberation was the organizing and political awakening of the woman worker to make common cause with the men of her class. Men and women of the working class needed to work together to overthrow a system oppressive to both.

In speeches and in the pages of *Gleichheit* (*Equality*), the organ of the socialist women's movement, which she edited until 1915, Zetkin would stress repeatedly that the major aim of the women's movement was to raise the class consciousness of women, to make them better soldiers in the struggle against capitalist society, and that the emancipation of women was tied to the emancipation of the working class as a whole. In practice, she had to struggle not only against capitalist society but also against socialist comrades; and though she often complained bitterly and loudly about the treatment of women within the party, she did not draw any new conclusions from her experiences or broaden her analysis.

For the organized socialist women's movement, Zetkin's 1889 pamphlet was the last attempt at a comprehensive analytical understanding of the oppression of women. New contributions to socialist theory on women would not be made until the emergence of a new radical women's movement in the late 1960s.[23]

ORGANIZED SOCIALISM AND WOMEN'S EMANCIPATION

Although socialist theory was clearly committed to women's emancipation, socialist men often expressed more ambivalent attitudes toward their female comrades. Socialist women who wanted to become activists in the class struggle had to contend with resistance not only from traditionalists within German society but from their socialist comrades as well.

Antifeminist attitudes within the working class expressed themselves in discussions of the woman question at party and trade union congresses. As has been mentioned, in the early years of the labor movement, women were seen as competitors in the labor market who took jobs away from men and depressed wages. Some socialist leaders insisted that women were retarding the whole progress of the working-class movement by providing employers with cheap, available labor. Despite Marx and Engels' recognition of the inevitability and desirability of women employed in social production, within the German Social Democratic movement the initial response was to try to keep women out of the labor force. In 1867, the General German Workers Congress passed the following resolution:

> The employment of women in the great industrial workshops is one of the most shocking abuses of our age. It is shocking because it causes the condition of the working class not to be improved but to be impaired, and it places the working population in a wretched condition through its destruction of the family.[24]

Many men within the working-class movement continued to maintain this attitude of hostility toward women's employment, not wanting to comprehend the implications of women employed outside the home in ever-increasing numbers. The extent of misunderstanding was exemplified by the comments of one spokesman at the First International in Geneva (1866), who understood the problem of women's employment to be related to that of prostitution. Socialism, he thought, would simply solve the problem by enabling every man to marry and thus providing every woman with a desirable and honorable livelihood.[25]

Despite the continuing debates, German Social Democracy formulated its official position on women working outside the home by 1869. At the party congress in Eisenach, it accepted the Marxist premise that more and more women would enter the labor force and that the hope of improving wages and working conditions through the elimination of cheap female labor was not realistic. Instead, Social Democrats argued, women had to be organized, their class consciousness raised, and their wages equalized. Only in this way could the general level of the working class be raised.[26] The trade unions continued to maintain an attitude of hostility toward women workers, and the opposing views on this question between the political and trade union branches of

Social Democracy became another one of the sources of division that eventually led to the much analyzed split of the working-class movement in Germany.

The debate was expanded at the party congress in Gotha in 1875 when radicals wanted to include women's suffrage in the party program, while conservatives feared that women were politically naive and would give their votes to reactionaries.[27] In a compromise solution, the Gotha program called for universal suffrage for all citizens, thereby including women without mentioning them specifically.[28] To satisfy the trade union elements, the Gotha congress also demanded the elimination of child labor and "unhealthy and improper" female labor (*Gesundheit und Sittlichkeit schädigende Frauenarbeit*).[29] The politicians' concept of what constituted proper female labor was based on prevailing bourgeois notions of femininity. The contempt for bourgeois values and life-styles as well as the feminist implications expressed by socialist theoreticians were not always shared by the rank and file, nor by the party and trade union leadership.

The years after the Gotha congress were significant in the working-class movement for the antisocialist laws passed by Bismarck, which made the Social Democratic Party illegal in Germany for twelve years (1878-1890). Those years were also significant for the more comprehensive articulation of the woman question in Bebel's *Woman under Socialism* in 1879 and Engels' *Origin of the Family* in 1884.

The year before the antisocialist laws were allowed to lapse, the beginnings of an organized women's movement emerged from discussions at the Paris International of 1889. Accepted and promoted officially by the SPD, an organized women's movement emerged, grew, and faltered, and then again grew in confronting social and legal obstacles to female political activism. Its first and foremost obstacle was the association and assembly laws (*Vereinsgesetze*) of many German states, which were designed to exclude women from political life and in some cases from any kind of public life whatsoever.[30]

The association laws and their enforcement differed from state to state. In Prussia, the largest and most powerful state

and the model for many other states, the laws prohibited
women from joining any kind of political organization. Wom-
en could not even attend meetings sponsored by political organizations, and violations could lead to the fining or disband-
ing of the offending organization. Under such conditions, a
women's organization connected to the Social Democratic
Party had some special problems. Fortunately, in the first five
years of the movement, the laws were not strictly enforced.

Before 1895, in the first phase of the Social Democratic
Women's Movement, the Prussian government left the decision
of whether or not a meeting was political to the discretion of
local police. Many meetings obviously organized by the SPD
were allowed to take place as long as they made a pretense of
being for educational or other nonpolitical purposes. Despite
the government's liberal enforcement of its reactionary laws,
the association laws seriously curtailed the political activity
and political effectiveness of women in the party. As a result
of the laws and possible police harassment, women were excluded from local party organizations, and the party became
increasingly wary of having women attend its meetings and
thereby risking fines or disbandment.[31] The effect of such re-
pression on the women themselves was to make socialist wom-
en generally more radical than their male comrades. For politically conscious and committed socialist women, there was to
be no chance for accommodation with the existing system. It
was best overthrown, they reasoned.

Notwithstanding all of these handicaps, the women's movement made some distinct progress between 1890 and 1895. At
the party congress in Halle (1890), the party approved the
founding of a journal geared to working women, *Die Arbeiterin*
(The Working Woman), later renamed *Gleichheit*, which was
to become the major theoretical organ of the German socialist
women's movement. In 1891, after years of hedging, the party
finally committed itself to "universal equal direct suffrage with
secret ballot for all citizens over twenty years of age without
distinction of sex."[32] The party program of 1891 also demanded
the abolition of all laws that discriminated against women and
placed them in an inferior position.[33] With this program, the

SPD became the first and, until after World War I, the only
political party in Germany to make a clear commitment to
women's rights.

The organized women's movement in these years was given
direction by Clara Zetkin and the Berlin Agitation Commission,
which consisted of seven women, including Zetkin. This small
group arranged for socialist speakers and organizers to tour
Germany and recruit working women to the socialist cause.
Circumventing the association laws, they organized educational
study groups for women where women were introduced to socialist ideology and instilled with the concept of class struggle.
With increasing activity came the increasing attention of the
state, and after a women's demonstration in 1893 against a
program of military expansion, the association laws began to
be more strictly enforced.[34] By 1895, the state governments
had succeeded in forcing the disbandment of the Berlin Agitation Commission, thereby effectively destroying the working
women's political movement.[35]

The second phase of the movement, 1895 to 1900, was a time
of diminished activism. Frustrated in their political activity, socialist women turned their attention to recruiting working wom-
en for the trade unions. While the unions were less than enthusiastic about working women, recruiting women into the unions
had been a long-held goal of Social Democrats. However, it was
not until political activity became impossible that serious efforts
were made in that direction. At the 1894 party congress, party
and trade union leaders decided that since the political organization of women had become difficult, the unions should now
take the initiative in bringing women into the working-class
movement.[36] As a result, while the number of women working
in industry and crafts increased from 940,000 to 1.4 million,
or by almost 50 percent, between 1895 and 1907, the number
of women in the trade unions increased by more than 2,700
percent, from 5,251 in 1894 to 136,939 in 1907.[37]

In addition to struggling with the antifeminist bias of their
socialist comrades and repressive laws, the socialist women's
movement in these years was also faced with an internal ideologic conflict. The conflict was personified in the struggle for

leadership between Clara Zetkin and Lily Braun and paralleled the division between Marxists and revisionists in the socialist movement as a whole. Clara Zetkin was a radical and doctrinaire Marxist whose ideological position never changed throughout her forty-four-year political career (1889-1933). As author of "Working Women and the Contemporary Woman Question" and as editor of *Gleichheit*, Zetkin was the ideologic guardian of the Marxist interpretation of women's emancipation. In her writing, she vehemently attacked all discussion of reform and compromise with existing society; she continually emphasized the concept of the class struggle and the overthrow of capitalist society. Her radicalism made it impossible for her to work with the bourgeois women's movement, which, like the socialist women's movement, was seeking to change conditions for women in German society. For Zetkin, of course, the feminist goal of making women strong and independent was only the first stage and preparation for the real struggle of creating a socialist society. Zetkin bitterly attacked bourgeois feminism at every opportunity and reminded socialist women that they had more in common with their working-class brothers than with bourgeois women.

Lily Braun, an attractive and inspiring orator, was a Prussian aristocrat turned socialist. She was initially welcomed into the women's movement by Zetkin, but by the end of the century, Braun's increasingly revisionist sentiments made the two women bitter enemies. Zetkin was eventually able to force Braun out of all decision-making positions in the movement, and by 1906 Braun bitterly withdrew from public life. Although radical at the beginning of her conversion to socialism, Braun gave up the concept of class struggle and came to believe that socialist women and bourgeois women could work together for a better world. She believed in the possibility of social reform "based on careful investigation of existing social relations"[38] and sought to orient the women's movement along this line. Zetkin responded that socialists could not afford to disperse their energies on reform efforts. Lily Braun was one of those rare socialist intellectuals who confronted the problem of women's domestic duties. For example, she called for the creation of communal households to relieve women of their family responsibilities. She correctly perceived that women's emancipation and human development could not proceed without some solution to this thorny problem.[39]

The reaction of working-class women to Braun's elaborate scheme of socialized family life remained cool. She was attacked for trying to divert the working class from its main political goal, for trying to reconcile the proletariat with existing society, and for destroying intimate family life for a barrack existence. Clara Zetkin responded to Braun's proposal as "the latest blossoming of utopianism in its most dangerous, opportunistic form."[40] In a series of articles in *Gleichheit*, Zetkin agreed that being wife, mother, and wage earner was a heavy burden but argued that change in the living conditions of women could not be realized in capitalist society. She characterized Braun's cooperative schemes as bourgeois reform work, reprimanded her for not distinguishing socialist from bourgeois concerns, and dismissed the proposal as having no relevance for the agitational efforts of female comrades.[41]

The prewar women's movement entered a new and third phase after 1900 as state governments again became more tolerant of women's political activities. In Prussia, women were allowed to attend political meetings as long as they were separated from men by a curtain or some other kind of partition. The year 1900 was also a watershed for the Social Democratic movement in general. Because laws before 1900 forbade party organization across state borders, the party necessarily had a loose, decentralized structure. Only after the repeal of these laws in 1900 did the SPD move toward the highly centralized and uniform party structure for which it has become so well known.[42] Change in the party structure also meant change for the women's movement within Social Democracy, and generally the change to a more centralized party structure would prove beneficial for women.

In the years between 1900 and 1908, the women's movement focused less on political education and more on discussion of current issues, such as protective legislation for working women and children, shorter hours and better working conditions, insurance programs for mothers, the education of children, and

political equality in the form of the vote and freedom of association.[43] In taking up these issues, women moved closer to the
reformist wing of the party, which sought social change within
existing bourgeois society.

In 1908, the association laws were finally repealed, women
were granted freedom of association in all of Germany, and the
Social Democratic Women's Movement entered its most expan-
sive phase, growing from 10,943 members in 1907 to 141,115 in
1913. Women could now be integrated into the regular party
structure, and all of their special organizations could cease to
exist. The leadership of the women's movement, however, correctly perceived that without special provisions and special organizations for women's participation, integration would become absorption and the articulation and struggle for women's
interests would be low on the list of SPD priorities. Clara Zetkin
knew that her power and influence would be diminished if wom-
en lost their special status within the party, and while she continued to proclaim her solidarity with socialist men in the class
struggle, within the party she fought for women's special interests.

Women did become members in the SPD but with special provisions. Their monthly dues were 20 *pfennig* as opposed to 30
pfennig for men,[44] the executive committee of every local SPD
organization was charged to elect at least one woman,[45] and
women were permitted to maintain their separate organizations
within the party. The party executive continued to maintain a
women's bureau (*Frauenbureau*), whose head also served on
the national executive committee. In addition, it was mandated
that an additional woman be regularly elected to the party executive. Despite some opposition, the women also continued their
separate biannual congresses and their for-women-only political
discussion groups.[46] *Gleichheit* also continued publication as the
special journal of the women's branch of German Social Democracy. By 1911, with women members of the SPD numbering well
over 100,000, Luise Zietz, a member of the executive committee,
proclaimed that women were beginning to acquire the feeling
of belonging in the party.

As the women's movement increased in membership and became somewhat more integrated into the party, it gradually

shifted from revolutionary radicalism toward reformism. In this the women's movement imitated the progress of the party as a whole. When the leadership represented few women, when they were oppressed by the state and limited in their participation in politics, they were consistently radical, but as they became responsible to greater numbers of working women and were offered the opportunity to work for reforms within bourgeois society, most, with the significant exception of Clara Zetkin, moved toward the revisionist wing of the party.[47]

This trend was completed by the division of the party's left and moderate wings precipitated by World War I. Consistently radical women such as Clara Zetkin left the Social Democratic Party to join the Independent Social Democratic Party (USPD) and later the Communist Party of Germany. The women who stayed with the majority socialist party modified their goals and views and gave the women's movement a conciliatory new direction that was eventually to undermine its radical theoretical tenets. The revolutionary theory of women's liberation, however, never changed to accommodate the new reformist practices. In this the women's movement also paralleled the party as a whole, which in theory remained committed to revolutionary socialism until after World War II.

There were some intellectual attacks on the Marxist theory of women's emancipation, which probably expressed the feelings of many socialist men but which certainly did not lead to reconceptualization of the role of women in the party or the future socialist society. These attacks were published in 1905 and 1917 in *Sozialistische Monatshefte*, the major revisionist socialist theoretical journal, by Edmund Fischer, who questioned the core of the Marxist thesis of the social productiveness of women and thus recalled the old antifeminist arguments of the labor movement. Fischer wrote:

The real core of the woman question is this: if the unalterable course of progress leads women into the labor force, and if that is to be welcomed and promoted because it brings about the reorganization of society, in which woman will become truly free and economically independent of man, will she thereby be emancipated? Or is the social labor of women something unnatural, socially unhealthy, one of the evils of capitalism, which should disappear with the end of capitalism. . . . The old view of emancipation which still haunts many heads, is, in my opinion, no longer justified today. The progress of female labor is not in the anticipated direction. The communal kitchens and households remain a utopian dream frustrated by the psychological make-up of mankind, man as well as woman . . . so-called woman's liberation goes against feminine and human nature in general, it is unnatural, and therefore impossible.[48]

Fischer believed that socialism should not take women out of the home, where they were fulfilling their natural and socially desirable role. Capitalism had driven women into wage labor; socialism would restore the natural order so that women could afford to devote themselves to home and family.[49]

In 1905, Fischer's article drew an angry and immediate response from Zetkin and other socialist women. However, when in 1917 Fischer again discussed his views in *Sozialistische Monatshefte*, hardly a word of protest was raised against him.[50] The German sociologist Werner Thoennessen concluded:

From the protocols of the Social Democratic Party Congresses and the women's congresses, one can conclude that the Fischer reaction against the theory of women's emancipation was no isolated example, but a symptom of its decline. The old theory was no longer formally attacked, but undermined directly through party politics and indirectly through the consequences of those policies within the party and society.[51]

What Thoennessen failed to note was that, in fact, the old theory continued to shape the thinking of Social Democratic women but that it was not particularly helpful in serving as a guide for strategy once the SPD and its women became committed to working for reform of capitalist society through parliamentary democracy.

The first quarter-century of the women's movement was characterized by the theoretical articulation of women's oppression and the growth of an organized movement under the leadership of Clara Zetkin. In this phase, the socialist women's movement remained theoretically radical but gradually moved toward revisionism in the ideological split developing within German socialism. World War I, which resulted in the division of the SPD, saw the completion of the process.

NOTES

1. For a discussion of how changing class relationships change the relations between the sexes, see Joan Kelly-Gadol, "The Social Relation of the Sexes: Methodological Implications of Women's History," *Signs: Journal of Women in Culture and Society* 1 (Summer, 1976): 809-823.

2. Charles Fourier, *Theorie des quatre mouvements, Oeuvres complètes*, 1: 195, quoted in George Lichtheim, *Origins of Socialism* (London, 1969), p. 37. Also see Lichtheim, pp. 35-37 and 69-70, for a discussion of Utopian socialism and the woman question, as well as Robert Neumann, "Socialism, the Family, and Sexuality: The Marxist Tradition and German Social Democracy before 1914" (Ph.D. dissertation, Northwestern University, 1972), pp. 6-30.

3. See Friedrich Engels, *Outline of a Critique of the National Economy* (1844), *The Condition of the Working Class in England* (1845), *The Origin of the Family, Private Property, and the State* (1884), and *Ten-Hour Bill* (1850); Karl Marx and Friedrich Engels, *The German Ideology* (1846) and *The Holy Family* (1845). For the collected comments of Marx on women, see Saul K. Padover, ed., *Karl Marx on Education, Women, and Children*, Karl Marx Library, vol. 6 (New York, 1975).

4. August Bebel, *Woman under Socialism* (New York, 1971); Clara Zetkin, *Die Arbeiterinnen und Frauenfrage der Gegenwart* (Berlin, 1889).

5. Karl Marx and Friedrich Engels, *The Communist Manifesto* (New York: International Publishers, 1973), pp. 26-28.

6. Engels, *Origin of the Family* (New York: International Publishers, 1971), p. 64. Engels' reasoning reflects his own nineteenth-century contradictions about women's sexuality more than prehistoric women's feelings about sex.

7. Ibid., p. 67.

8. For some twentieth-century defenders of the existence of mother-

right, see Robert Briffault, *The Mothers* (New York, 1927); Evelyn Reed, *Woman's Evolution* (New York, 1975); Sarah B. Pomeroy, *Goddesses, Whores, Wives, and Slaves: Women in Classical Antiquity* (New York, 1976).

9. Engels, *Origin of the Family*, p. 75.

10. Simone de Beauvoir, *The Second Sex* (New York, 1961), pp. 48-55; Shulamith Firestone, *The Dialectic of Sex* (New York, 1971); Juliet Mitchell, *Woman's Estate* (New York, 1973). For a critique of modern radical feminists from a Marxist perspective, see Charnie Guettel, *Marxism and Feminism* (Toronto, 1974).

11. De Beauvoir, *The Second Sex*, p. 71.

12. Ibid., p. 75.

13. It would be beyond the scope of this study to go into detail on the controversy among anthropologists of Morgan's work in general and his thesis of the matriarchy in particular. For a critique of Morgan's thesis, see Gordon Childs, *Social Evolution* (London, 1952), pp. 6-11, 28. For a discussion to reconsider Morgan's work if not his conclusion of the matriarchy, see Emmanuel Terray, *Marxism and 'Primitive Societies"* (New York, 1972). For a staunch defense, see Evelyn Reed, "Introduction" to *Origin of the Family* (New York: International Publishers, 1971); Evelyn Reed, *Problems of Women's Liberation* (New York, 1972), pp. 12-27.

14. Engels, *Origin of the Family*, p. 79.

15. Ibid., p. 82.

16. Bebel's book has been published under a number of titles. The first German edition of 1879 was entitled *Die Frau und der Sozialismus;* the second, or 1883 edition, had the title *Die Frau in der Vergangenheit, Gegenwart und Zukunft.* The latter was translated into English by H. B. Adams as *Women in the Past, Present, and Future* (1893). A second English edition appeared in 1910 under the title *Woman and Socialism.* The most recent English publication is that by Schocken Books in 1971 entitled *Woman under Socialism.* Of the German-language editions, the most recent one is that published in East Berlin in 1962 entitled *Die Frau und der Sozialismus.*

17. Hilde Lion, *Zur Soziologie der Frauenbewegung* (Berlin, 1926), pp. 35-38.

18. August Bebel, *Woman under Socialism* (New York, 1971), pp. 6, 9. The emphasis is Bebel's.

19. Ibid., p. 5.

20. Ibid., p. 121.

21. Ibid., pp. 343-344.

22. For a discussion of labor's attitudes toward women, see Ibid., pp. 40-45.

23. New theoretical works on women from a socialist perspective in-

clude Sheila Rowbotham, *Woman's Consciousness, Man's World* (Middlesex, England, 1973); Juliet Mitchell, *Woman's Estate* (New York, 1973); Margaret Benston, "The Political Economy of Women's Liberation," *Monthly Review* 21 (September, 1969): 13-27.

24. Wilhelm Schroeder, *Handbuch der sozialdemokratischen Parteitage von 1863-1909* (Munich, 1910), p. 463.

25. *Bericht über die Verhandlungen des 3. Vereintages deutscher Arbeitervereine* (Geneva, 1866), p. 151.

26. *Protokoll des Allgemeinen Deutschen Sozialdemokratischen Arbeiterkongresses* (Eisenach; Leipzig, 1869).

27. *Protokoll* (1875), quoted in *Die Ersten Sozialistenkongresse*, p. 109. When women finally got the vote in 1918, the conservatives seemed to be proven right.

28. Ibid., p. 111.

29. Ibid., p. 69.

30. For a comprehensive discussion of the German association laws, see Jacqueline Strain, "Feminism and Political Radicalism in the German Social Democratic Movement, 1890-1914" (Ph.D. dissertation, University of California, 1964), pp. 55-69.

31. Ibid., p. 65.

32. *Protokoll* (1891), p. 5. In German the resolution reads: "Allgemeines gleiches direktes Wahl-und Stimmrecht mit geheimer Stimmabgabe aller über 20 Jahre alten Reichangehörigen ohne Unterschied des Geschlechts für alle Wahlen und Abstimmungen."

33. Ibid.

34. Strain, "Feminism and Political Radicalism," p. 96.

35. Ibid., p. 95.

36. Ibid., p. 110.

37. Juergen Kuczynski, *Die Geschichte der Lage der Arbeiter unter dem Kapitalismus* (Berlin, 1963), 18:105.

WORKERS IN INDUSTRY AND CRAFTS, 1875-1907

YEAR	MALE WORKERS*	PERCENT	FEMALE WORKERS*	PERCENT
1875	2.64	49.1%	0.49	9.2%
1882	3.12	51.9%	0.58	9.6%
1895	4.59	57.6%	0.94	11.8%
1907	6.53	60.5%	1.40	12.9%

*In millions.

Werner Thoennessen, *Frauenemanzipation. Politik und Literatur der Deutschen Sozialdemokratie* (Frankfurt/M, 1969), p. 62.

FEMALE UNION MEMBERS, 1875-1907

YEAR	FEMALE UNION MEMBERS	PERCENT
1875	—	—
1882	—	—
1895	6,697	2.5%
1907	136,929	7.3%

38. Jean Helen Quataert, "The German Socialist Women's Movement, 1890-1918: Issues, Internal Conflicts, and Main Personages" (Ph.D. dissertation, University of California at Los Angeles, 1974), p. 229.

39. Lily Braun, *Frauenarbeit und Hauswirtschaft* (Berlin, 1901).

40. Documents IISH.NL Kautsky, KD XXIII, 339 (Stuttgart, May 16, 1901), quoted in Quataert, "The German Socialist Women's Movement," p. 257.

41. *Gleichheit* (June 19, 1901), p. 97; (July 3, 1901), pp. 105-106; (July 17, 1901), pp. 113-114.

42. Strain, "Feminism and Political Radicalism," p. 163. To circumvent the laws, the SPD before 1900 had a system of *Vertrauensperson*, who was a local representative for the party. After 1900, they gradually did away with the *Vertrauensperson* in favor of a more centralized hierarchical system. As the association laws in many states would have frozen women out of the party, they kept both systems in some areas. With this dual system, more and more women *Vertrauenspersonen* were elected.

43. Ibid., pp. 181-229.

44. *Protokoll* (1908), p. 233.

45. *Protokoll* (1909), p. 235.

46. Strain, "Feminism and Political Radicalism," p. 238.

47. Ibid., pp. 230-263.

48. Edmund Fischer, "Die Frauenfrage," *Sozialistische Monatshefte* 1 (1905): 258-262.

49. Ibid., p. 262.

50. Edmund Fischer, "Tendenzen der Frauenarbeit," *Sozialistische Monatshefte* 2 (1917): 545. An exception was a criticism of Fischer in a book that appeared two years later: Wally Zepler, *Sozialismus und Frauenfrage* (Berlin, 1919).

51. Thoennessen, *Frauenemanzipation*, p. 119.

2

THE CHANGING CHARACTER OF THE SOCIAL DEMOCRATIC WOMEN'S MOVEMENT

WORLD WAR I brought about dramatic changes in Germany and divided the nearly forty-year-old German Social Democratic Party into two and then three socialist parties. The changes within the party and the course and nature of the war also forced a reorientation in the socialist women's movement. The radical orientation and emphasis on class struggle that had characterized the prewar movement were not carried into the postwar era.

The reasons for this are complex and multifaceted, and they mirror the course of German Social Democracy in general during the Weimar Republic. The change from a revolutionary to a reformist party was undoubtedly the most significant factor causing a reorientation of the women's movement. However, it is not the purpose of this study to repeat the discussion of that well-documented phenomenon but rather to examine the specific instances that were at once a reflection and an affirmation of that change within the women's movement.[1] These instances include: the loss of Clara Zetkin, the guiding spirit of the prewar Social Democratic Women's Movement, to the Communist Party; the reordering of priorities by socialist women initiated by the great human needs of the war as well as the psychological trauma of the war itself; the legalistic equality that the 1918 November Revolution gave to German women and, according to Zetkin's replacement, Marie Juchacz, made German women "the freest in the world";[2] and the vote and constitutional equality, which put the emphasis on

new responsibility as well as new rights and gave Social Democratic women the opportunity to struggle for equality through
the existing political structure—bourgeois, male-dominated parliamentary democracy.

The changes are also rooted in the history of the Social Democratic Women's Movement. Social Democratic women insisted
that they were not feminists (*Frauenrechtlerinnen*), claiming
that feminists were primarily bourgeois women who emphasized
the struggle as primarily one between men and women. Clara
Zetkin always emphasized class and party solidarity, with socialist men and women fighting together for a better world that
would include, among other things, full social and political
equality for women. Nevertheless, Clara Zetkin also realized that
women were faced with a struggle against men—both capitalist
and socialist. She was fully aware that many men in the party
lacked a commitment to women's equality, particularly when it
left the realm of the abstract and applied to their wives or daughters. While Zetkin prepared women for the coming class struggle,
she also fought for recognition and support for the women's
cause within the party. In short, she carried on the struggle on
two levels: together with men for the cause of the socialist future
and against men in the party for autonomy and power.

This contradiction, upon which women in the 1920s and succeeding generations of politically conscious and active women
would flounder, was balanced successfully by Clara Zetkin. Her
dynamic personality was a factor in her ability to wage the simul-
taneous struggle with and against socialist men, but more important were the objective conditions of socialist politics prior
to World War I. If women were to be politically active at all, they
were forced by the association laws into separate organizations,
which had the effect of helping them understand their interests
as *women* and which eliminated the possibility of co-optation.
Furthermore, as long as the SPD was the party in opposition,
without much possibility of becoming a ruling party, the posture
of any special-interest group within German Social Democracy
was not so critical. Playing the role of critics of Wilhelminian
society, the SPD could only benefit from the agitation of its
women. Once the party was in power, or had the possibility of

political power, issues of women's equality would become more troublesome. Historically persuaded of class and party solidarity, women would also not be inclined to struggle against their socialist comrades who were directing the course of the nation. Agitation could be encouraged in Wilhelminian society, but once the party was in power, patience and conformity to the interests of the party as a whole would be counseled.

THE CHANGING LEADERSHIP

With the departure of Clara Zetkin in 1917, the Social Democratic Women's Movement lost its most dynamic and eloquent leader. No Social Democratic women during the 1920s ever achieved her stature. From the time Zetkin joined the German socialist movement as a young girl to the end of her long life, she was an unswerving Marxist, a faithful believer in doctrinaire scientific socialism. World War I, which created crises of conscience for many Social Democrats, presented no problem for Zetkin.[3] In the midst of the most intense nationalism, she remained a staunch internationalist. Shortly before the advent of war, when nationalistic fervor was at a high pitch in Germany, she called upon the working class to prevent war,[4] and once it had broken out, she advised her followers not to fall prey to nationalistic chauvinism but to keep working-class internationalism alive.[5] She reminded those who saw the war as a great clash of opposing cultures that German culture, and especially the great classic literary epoch, owed much to French and English influences.[6]

In a December 3, 1914, letter, she recalled her personal sense of betrayal when news of the Social Democratic capitulation to nationalism and their vote for war reached her: "I thought I would go mad or have to commit suicide. I was very ill for a month, and even now I am not well."[7] After being restrained in her editorial comments in the first months, she finally wrote her analysis in *Gleichheit* that the war was an internal victory of the capitalist ruling class over the socialist parties. With dismay, she noted the general capitulation of the socialist parties of other European nations, of which only the Independent

Labour Party of Britain and the Social Democrats of Serbia and Russia abstained from participating in the events that led to the outbreak and continuation of World War I.[8]

Zetkin's editorializing became increasingly offensive to the Social Democratic leadership, which had agreed to conclude a temporary peace with the state for the duration of the war (*Burgfrieden*). In May, 1917, the party executive finally fired her as editor of *Gleichheit*, with the official explanation that the journal under Zetkin had become too theoretical and not popular enough among working-class women. It was a familiar criticism, which had been leveled at her many times, but for a quarter-century she had been successful in maintaining *Gleichheit*'s political and theoretical focus, refusing to turn it into a working-class version of bourgeois women's magazines, featuring recipes, fashions, and sentimental fiction.[9]

Zetkin's replacement, Marie Juchacz, announced *Gleichheit*'s new editorial policy in its June 8, 1917, edition, and the real objections to Clara Zetkin became very clear. *Gleichheit* would now put national interests above international. A strong Germany, its new editor announced, was a prerequisite for a strong working-class movement.[10] In addition, *Gleichheit* was now to be a unifying, reconciling influence that would not attempt to make the women's movement into a separate organization within the party.[11] Hinting at the executive committee's displeasure at the maintenance of autonomy under Zetkin's leadership, Marie Juchacz indicated that the women's movement would now follow a different course.

With the split in the party and the departure of the more radical membership, a radical socialist women's movement no longer had a home in the SPD, but the tradition continued briefly in the first splinter group, the Independent Social Democratic Party (USPD), until its dissolution in 1922. For some time after leaving the SPD and *Gleichheit*, Zetkin edited a women's page for the USPD in the *Leipziger Volkszeitung*, but when the left wing of the newly formed USPD split to join the newly formed Communist Party (KPD), Zetkin went with them. In the Communist Party, she was to be an influential voice, but she did not head up a separate women's movement. At the 1920 congress which joined the two parties, Zetkin was there to explain the role of women. In much the same terms she had used at the 1889 International, Zetkin reiterated the classic socialist idea that the basis of all oppression, including women's, was private property:

> The Communist party does not have to revise its basic concept of the woman question. It maintains that the woman question is not separate [from the working-class question] and cannot be solved in a capitalist economy and bourgeois order by reforms in favor of the female sex. It is our opinion that the woman question is only a part of the greater social question, and can be solved only when the proletariat smashes the capitalist system and builds the communist system in the joint struggle of all exploited and oppressed without regard to sex.[12]

Throughout the 1920s, Zetkin continued her work to win women for the revolutionary struggle and to persuade them that their interests could best be served through the ideology of revolutionary socialism, as embodied by the Communist Party. She became a fervent admirer of Lenin and Russian communism and one of the important links between the German and Russian Communist parties. She made frequent trips to Russia, where she met with Lenin and was inspired to describe him as one of the foremost leaders in the battle for the emancipation of women.[13]

She also praised the Russian Communist Party for being the only party to secure for women full social and human rights and for having fully and equally integrated women into the party organization.[14] The early years of the Russian Revolution were, of course, an inspiration to activist women everywhere as they noted the social advances that Russian women were making. Their own experiences with Communist leaders must have been less inspiring. Robert Wheeler has pointed out the disappointment of women with the attitude of the leadership at the Third International, where the woman question was not discussed for lack of time.[15]

Following the long career of Clara Zetkin, one is struck by her unswerving steadfastness and untiring devotion to her cause. Her writings toward the end of her life, although filled more with the rhetoric of revolutionary communism, are in content no different from her writings of 1889. Throughout the 1920s, she continued to make her presence felt through essays and speeches and as a delegate of the Communist Party to the Reichstag.

She also did not hesitate to criticize the German Communist Party for not doing more to involve women. Especially during the revolutionary November days, she deplored the fact that at the first *Räte Kongress* (congress of the revolutionary councils, which appeared as an alternative to government all over Germany), there was only one woman representative. She pointed to the importance of drawing women into the revolutionary struggle and chided the Communists for their failure to perceive this.[16] She also continued to insist on special training and education for women within the party. Women could not be treated the same as men. Even in a communist society, biological and psychological differences had to be taken into account and special provisions made.[17] For the majority Social Democratic women, Clara Zetkin became a somewhat embarrassing figure, whose past dedication had to be honored but whose continuing existence was best ignored.[18]

Zetkin's replacement in the Social Democratic Women's Movement was Marie Juchacz, a woman more in tune with the changing character of the party. The difference between the personalities of Zetkin and Juchacz is exemplary of the differences between the prewar and postwar movements. While Zetkin was a well-educated, self-confident, fiery revolutionary, Juchacz was a reticent bureaucrat from a working-class background with little formal education. Juchacz found her place in the world and purpose in life through the party. She personified the phenomenon of the outsider who becomes the unwitting defender of the status quo even while working to change it. The vision of the socialist revolution remained the source of Zetkin's energy and purpose; for Juchacz it was her position in the party that gave her life meaning and purpose.

Born in 1879 in Landsberg, a provincial village in Branden-burg, Marie Gohlke Juchacz came from a lower-middle-class family that had slipped into the ranks of the proletariat when the father lost his job for participating in a strike. Marie's father, brother, and sister all became active members of the SPD, and it was through her brother, Otto, that Marie was introduced to socialism with Bebel's *Woman under Socialism*.[19]

At age 14, her formal education ended, and like most work-ing-class girls in Landsberg, she found a job at the local factory. There she learned firsthand of the plight of working-class wom-en, who often had to support children and sick husbands on pitifully inadequate wages. As much as her identification with the plight of factory workers, her own need to grow and develop intellectually led her to the party.[20]

In 1903, she married and eventually gave birth to two chil-dren. Her marriage was unhappy, and shortly after the birth of her second child, she left Landsberg and her husband to join her brother Otto and sister Elizabeth in Berlin. There a close personal and working relationship developed between the two sisters, and together they worked effectively until Elizabeth's sudden death in 1933. During those first days in Berlin, Elizabeth cared for the children while Marie worked as a seamstress. Their evenings were spent organizing reading clubs for socialist women. Gradually Marie moved up in the party, where she was valued for her hard work and discretion in never taking a controversial stand.

Seven years after her move to Berlin, Juchacz attained her first paid position in the SPD as party secretary in Cologne. Her assignment was to recruit working women for the party, which was no easy task in Catholic Cologne. When war broke out, the SPD's decision to support it apparently gave her some personal difficulty, but typically she refused to take a public stand. Even much later, she refused to reveal her opinion on the subject, maintaining that it was not her place to offer opinions on any-thing not directly related to her work.[21]

In the midst of the party crisis in 1916, Friedrich Ebert called her to Berlin and asked her to replace Luise Zietz as secretary for women's affairs (*Frauensekretär*) in the party executive.

Modestly, she claimed to feel unprepared to assume the position of Zietz, an outspoken activist and long-time party member, but upon Ebert's urging, she accepted.

When Juchacz arrived in Berlin, she found a shattered organization, with many members and most leaders having left for the newly formed USPD. Whatever her initial hesitations, however, she did her job well enough to retain the position until the SPD was dissolved in 1933 after the National Socialist seizure of power. She presided over women's affairs at a time when female membership in the Party was expanding to reach a high of 230,000 members by 1931.[22] The expansion of membership under Juchacz's leadership continued a trend begun after the lapse of the association laws and interrupted only by World War I and the great inflation. The expanding female membership presented both an opportunity for the leadership to demand a greater voice for women within the party and a conservative influence channeling concerns into reforms that would alleviate the hardships of everyday life for the working-class woman and mother. Juchacz responded to this situation by founding the *Arbeiterwohlfahrt*, a wide-ranging working-class welfare organization that dealt with the needs of working-class families, especially women and children. Many, including her nephew and biographer, Fritzmichael Roehl, saw this as her greatest work. With the creation of a new organization, women could be politically active and useful, without challenging the power of men. Her creation of the *Arbeiterwohlfahrt* was another indication that Juchacz would provide a different style of leadership from that of Clara Zetkin. When in 1919 Juchacz was elected to the Reichstag and became the first woman to address a German parliamentary assembly, Friedrich Stampfer wrote in *Vorwärts*, the party's daily newspaper: "With Marie Juchacz, we have a new and totally different kind of woman. Gone is the era when the activists of the women's movement believed that they had to prove their equality by taking on male characteristics."[23]

Although Juchacz remained a reticent and private person who tried to avoid controversy, she was a major force in shaping the character of the Social Democratic Women's Movement in the 1920s. Despite her discretion and loyalty, and perhaps because of her role as leader of the women's movement, there are indications that she was not accepted in the inner circle, the party executive. When in 1933 the National Socialist victory forced the Social Democratic leadership to leave Germany and the executive committee fled to Prague, Juchacz was not asked to accompany them, and her biographer has indicated that she was to remain bitter over this for the rest of her life. Typically, she made no public statement and left no record of the incident.

After years of precarious existence, first in the Saar and later in Alsace, Marie Juchacz finally fled to the United States in 1941. At first deeply depressed about the prospect of making a new life for herself at age 62 in a country whose language was foreign to her and whose people had no use for her special skills, she gradually adapted, learned the language, and eventually became active in welfare work in New York City. In 1949 she returned to Germany to work for the American occupation and to resume her work with the *Arbeiterwohlfahrt*. Before she died in 1956, she finished a book of short biographical sketches of some of the leading women in the Social Democratic movement between 1890 and 1933. Published by the party press under the title *Sie lebten für eine bessere Welt*, Berlin, 1955 (*They Lived for a Better World*), she hoped that these sketches would enlighten and inspire a new generation of Social Democratic women.

In many ways, *Sie lebten für eine bessere Welt* was Marie Juchacz's most feminist statement. It was feminist in that it portrayed with great affection and respect 29 strong, determined women as role models for a new generation of politically conscious and active women. In the introduction, Juchacz wrote:

> After the last lost war [World War II], all of us, men as well as women, were faced with new problems, which we attempted to solve with zeal and courage. But we, and especially the younger ones among us, lack that which makes the solution of any kind of problem always easier: a guide, an example— many examples! We have a treasure of tradition, which lies hidden away. . . . We should bring that tradition to life, we should find the spirit which moved the socialists of the past to their great accomplishments. We must attempt to under-

stand and learn from them. Especially we women in our
present need and distress should know that before us, bold
women fought gladly and fearlessly for their human rights
and women's rights. . . .[24]

The women Juchacz sketched in brief portraits of no more
than four to five pages all fought for women's rights *and* socialism.[25] Women who remained with the SPD as well as those who
left for the USPD and the KPD are presented. Clara Zetkin is
portrayed as a woman of great intellect with a gift for oratory,
who may not have been greatly loved by socialists; but, Juchacz
wrote, "Social Democratic women owe Clara Zetkin a debt of
gratitude. The fact that she took a path different from our own
does not change that."[26] Rosa Luxemburg, who also left the
party, is described as a brilliant, warm, passionate human being
who was to be admired for her articulate convictions, even if
they differed from those of the mainstream party.[27]

In the introduction, Juchacz wrote that she did not want to
present these women as "heroines" but rather "as people such
as you and I," who, "through economic and social developments, became conscious of their deprivations and were pulled
into the struggles of their time."[28] Juchacz's strong affection
and admiration for these women, however, is apparent in every
portrait and makes them, if not "heroines," then shining examples of purposeful and courageous lives. Most of them came
from working-class backgrounds and overcame obstacles of pov-
erty, lack of education, and often poor health to work selflessly,
energetically, with great intelligence and resourcefulness, for
women and for socialism.

NEW DIRECTIONS AND PRIORITIES

With the split in the party and the more conservative direction
of the SPD and with new leadership in the women's movement,
the priorities and emphasis for women changed. As significant
as the political and bureaucratic changes in the party structure
was the experience of war itself, which changed women's per-
ceptions and priorities. Social Democratic women's participa-

tion in the war effort as workers and as organizers of relief work was a significant factor in changing the consciousness of many women. The emphasis on social welfare work, for example, which was one of the distinguishing characteristics of the postwar movement, grew naturally out of the work into which socialist women were drawn during the war. When human needs were greater than ever before due to the dislocation of war and when state institutions failed to meet those needs, the women's organizations, both socialist and bourgeois, stepped in to provide relief.

Clara Zetkin had preached a contempt for welfare work that sought only to bind the wounds inflicted by a chaotic capitalist system, but in 1914 even Clara Zetkin did not suggest that the class struggle and the socialist revolution might be advanced by allowing the pressing human needs at home to go unanswered. In the September 4, 1914, issue of *Gleichheit*, Zetkin called for an unprecedented cooperation between socialist and bourgeois women to ease the pain of suffering women and children.[29] Luise Zietz, another radical socialist leader who joined the USPD in 1917, described how the special needs of war were helping to define women's new role in social and community work.[30] The same Luise Zietz, as a parliamentary deputy in the 1920s, warned women not to allow themselves to be relegated to certain service areas, advising that the interests of women needed to be represented not only in health, education, and welfare, which perhaps appeared to be natural areas for women's involvement, but also in fiscal and foreign policies.[31]

Prior to World War I, social welfare work had been the domain of bourgeois women, who had seen it as a means of helping women become involved in life outside the home. This was not quite so conservative as it seems today, when welfare work has become "women's work." In Germany in the late nineteenth and early twentieth centuries, it was still frowned upon for the wives and daughters of the middle class to engage in this kind of work, and only the most daring and independent women did so. Because welfare work required some education, working-class women had no access to it prior to 1914.

During World War I, socialist and bourgeois women worked together for the first time, and although there was some friction, a precedent for a closer cooperation between them was established. Socialist women did not have the expertise, education, and experience of middle-class women in welfare work but considered their contribution especially valuable because they could relate better to needy working-class women. In class-bound Germany, that was undoubtedly very true. The cooperation between bourgeois and socialist women in welfare work also led to cooperation between the two groups in the peace movement. Both groups participated in the International Women's Day in Switzerland in March, 1915, which called for an end to war.[32]

Though the wartime emphasis on social welfare work was in itself not negative, it later became a convenient way to channel the energies of socially conscious women and to divert them from pressing their own claims for more rights and greater participation in the Social Democratic Party and German society. In the meantime, however, the women's movement made progress as many women became involved in community work for the first time. Consequently, it made them socially and politically more aware and conscious of the plight of women. In other respects, the war also changed the status of women. For example, attitudes toward unmarried mothers and illegitimate children were liberalized. Since the turn of the century, authorities in Germany had been concerned about the declining birth rate, and the slaughter of young German men during the war increased this concern. Consequently, all children were considered valuable to the state, and protection of mothers, wed and unwed, expanded during the war to reflect this attitude.

The war was also significant for opening jobs and professions previously closed to women, and they became more independent and self-confident as a result of their work experience. Although postwar attempts were made to reverse this trend, some of its effects on the consciousness of women could not be erased.[33]

POLITICAL EQUALITY

During the war, Social Democratic women stood behind their men and supported the war effort. As did the Social Democratic

Party, they concluded a temporary peace with the prevailing powers and did not press their cause. However, as the end approached, women again found their voice and this time with new confidence and determination brought about by their experiences. When the question was debated in the parliament in July, 1918, and again in October, 1918, only the SPD was prepared to vote for women's suffrage. The Center Party and the other bourgeois parties took a reactionary stand, insisting that now less than ever was it the time for equality, that women had more important work to do at home and in the family.[34] Again men insisted that women were to be the healers and binders of wounds, but they were not to have a say in the political processes that inflicted those wounds. Men were not only opposed to women's suffrage but expressed a misogyny and general fear of women in authority in the debates on political equality with comments such as, "In our fatherland, among our manly people, it should be impossible for a civil servant of high or low degree, be it a professor or a mailman, to have to take orders from a woman."[35] While the debate went on, the old regime was collapsing. With the precedent of their wartime cooperation in welfare work, women of all political persuasions joined together in October, 1918, to demand political equality.[36] A few weeks later, the November Revolution swept the Social Democrats into power, and women were granted the vote. One of the first pronouncements of the provisional government read: "All elections for public offices, based on proportional systems of representation, are now to be executed through equal, direct, secret suffrage for all persons, male and female, twenty years old or older."[37] Social Democratic women were to say later that women were granted the vote "by the grace of men." The new cooperation and determination shown by women's groups was, in their opinion, not the significant factor that brought them political equality; and thus the events of November, 1918, reinforced the old belief that the goals of Social Democratic women were best met by solidarity with the SPD and men of their class and not with feminist groups. Social Democratic women, with few exceptions, did not combine forces with other women's groups during the Weimar Republic, but the divisions separating the two groups were never again so sharply defined as they had been in Zetkin's day.

In the spring of 1919, German women went to the polls for the first time to vote for their representatives to the national assembly, which was to meet at Weimar to formulate the constitution for the new democratic republic. Not only did women vote for the first time, but because of the deaths of so many German men, they were a decided majority at the polls.[38] Overwhelmingly they voted for the SPD. Despite a large turnout, the problem of the woman as citizen was already apparent in that first election. A much larger percentage of women under age 25 voted as compared to men, while more women over age 25 stayed home as compared to men over age 25. It would not be unreasonable to conclude that family responsibilities and tradition kept a large percentage of women over 25 away from the polls.

Of 421 delegates sent to the national assembly, 41 were women, with the largest delegation coming from the SPD. Of the party's 165 delegates, 22, or 13.3 percent, were women.[39] In general, those Social Democratic women sent to the national assembly were middle-aged, from working-class families, had grown up under difficult circumstances, and, with a few exceptions, had not enjoyed the benefits of a higher education. Of the twenty-two, two were teachers, four were saleswomen (a trained position in Germany), and the rest were factory workers, servants, seamstresses, and housewives. All had years of party experience. Despite their party work, however, they felt timid and uneasy in the parliament and were glad to follow the lead of the men. Those women who had been the most vocal leaders in the fight for women's rights before the war were not part of the SPD delegation.[40]

In great contrast to the intellectual aggressiveness and experience of a Clara Zetkin, one of the delegates described her impressions of the work of women in the national assembly in the following way:

Filled with the greatness of their responsibility, women took up their new tasks for the first time in lovely Weimar . . .

most of them must have felt timid and anxious. Step by step,
we had to feel our way into the work. Often deep despondency
was ready to overcome us; for we came with such great hopes
and often they were disappointed. We were used to step in and
work practically wherever the need arose. Often the long discussions of single questions seemed useless. Gradually at first,
but then more surely we worked our way in.[41]

Even more telling of the mood of the women and an indication of the direction the new women's movement was to take
was the speech by Marie Juchacz before the national assembly.
In the first address of a woman before a German parliament,
Marie Juchacz stressed that women were going to work within
the framework of the party; they were not going to have a
separate organization. The woman question, she maintained, no
longer existed in the old sense of the word. Women now had the
same means at their command as men to fight for their social,
political, and economic rights. She did not mention that women
might have special problems that prevented them from exercising
those rights, although she certainly was aware of that. Juchacz
stressed instead that political rights and a new social role would
not change women. Stepping into the political arena, they
would not lose their femininity, she assured her audience. Then
she enumerated the various areas of public life that she felt
were especially well suited for women:

> The whole area of social politics [*Sozialpolitik*], including
> maternal protection[*Mutterschutz*], infant and child welfare
> must become in the widest sense a special area for women.
> The housing question, preventive medicine, child care, un-
> employment insurance are areas in which the female sex
> has a special interest and is especially well suited.[42]

Twice in her address she specifically mentioned the special cre-
dentials and interests of the woman as mother. This was indicative of the way the party was to view and appeal to women
during the Weimar Republic. "Vote for the SPD for the future
of your children" was a common campaign slogan designed to

appeal to women. The SPD also liked to stress the motherly qualities of their female politicians. Marie Juchacz was enough of a socialist to know that political equality did not mean an automatic translation into social and economic equality. Much work was needed to translate constitutional equality into real equality, she told her audience.[43]

The only objection to Marie Juchacz's designation of social welfare areas of public life as the special sphere of women came from Luise Zietz, a former leader of Social Democratic women, now in the Reichstag as a delegate of the USPD. Luise Zietz cited the danger of relegating women to special areas of public life. She protested that the political equality of women meant that women would be active and work beside men in all areas of public life.[44]

In general, Social Democratic women were satisfied with the new constitution, which went into effect on August 14, 1919. Disagreements over individual paragraphs of the constitution formed along party lines rather than along sex lines. Social Democratic women took no position that was not supported or endorsed by the party in general.

The Weimar constitution laid the basis for a modern democratic welfare state. It provided the theoretical basis for a new position for women in society. It was no wonder many Social Democratic women were optimistic. Those articles of the new constitution which specifically applied to women stated:

¶ 109. All Germans are equal before the law. Men and women have basically the same rights and duties of citizenship.

¶ 119. Marriage as the basis of family life and providing the maintenance and increase of the nation stands under the special protection of the constitution. It is based on the equality of both sexes.

The health, maintenance, and social promotion of the family is the task of the state and the community. Families with numerous children have the right of subsidies to ensure economic equality.

Mothers have the right to expect the care and protection of the state.

¶ 121. Illegitimate children have the right by law to the same physical, psychological, and social conditions necessary for their development as legitimate children.

¶ 128. Public offices are open to all citizens without exception according to law and their abilities and service. All exceptions against female civil servants are null and void.[45]

Mathilde Wurm, a major critic of the SPD's attitudes toward women, noted that the constitution was born out of the spirit of a bourgeois class society, not out of that of a socialist republic. Women's chains were loosened through the constitution, she said, but they were not sprung.[46] She noted that paragraph 119 affirmed the traditional Christian view of marriage as the basis for the state and did not conform to the socialist view of marriage as a private relationship.[47]

Social Democratic women at the national assembly did not object to the basic assumptions made by the constitution. They did object to some points. They considered the word "basically" in paragraph 109 a limitation on women. They also wanted to expand the rights of illegitimate children in regard to rights of inheritance and name of the father but had to compromise on the wording of paragraph 121.

The thoughts of Social Democratic women at the national assembly were summarized and published in a collection of essays in 1920 entitled *Frauenstimmen aus der Nationalversammlung*, Berlin, 1920 *(Women's Voices from the National Assembly)*. In this collection, each delegate expressed her major concerns. It is perhaps a better source for the opinions and ideas of Social Democratic women than the records of the national assembly itself, where Social Democratic women were hesitant to speak. Most of them expressed a clear awareness that equality still needed to be fought for, but were confident that within the party and through the party their interests would be promoted. They continued to identify themselves more with their social class than with women in general. Socialism through democracy they cited as their goal. Social Democratic women and bourgeois women might be able to travel some way together, as they had during the war, but eventually their class interests would force them apart.[48]

Again, one of the most common themes found in *Frauenstimmen* centered around the woman as mother. Marie Juchacz wrote that through political equality and the political work of women would finally come an appreciation of motherhood as a service to the people and the state. Out of the proper appreciation of the service of mothers to the state would come maternity and child care and other generous social programs.[49] Reform of marriage and divorce laws also interested Social Democratic women. Marie Juchacz and her politically active sister Elizabeth Roehl had both been divorced and faced with caring for their children alone and had a keen interest in this subject.

In conclusion, what these women hoped to do was to provide a social basis for the independent action of women. Recognizing that women were always going to be mothers, that they were going to bear the primary burden and responsibility for the care and education of children, they wanted through social programs to compensate women for their biologic burden. Political, social, and economic equality could become meaningful only if society compensated women; only then would women dare to act independently and begin to identify their interests, where these conflicted with the interests of men. Ideally, the struggle for equality as well as comprehensive social programs should progress simultaneously. Unfortunately, in the 1920s, the latter would be emphasized at the expense of the former. Though the focus on social welfare work tended to distract women from the struggle for equality, the emphasis on motherhood as a social issue was truly progressive. The call for programs to alleviate the burden of the woman as mother placed Marie Juchacz and the Social Democratic Women's Movement in line with radical feminists, who, through the *Mutterschutz* movement, had been working for more enlightened sexual attitudes, birth control, abortion, and support for pregnant women irrespective of their marital status since the turn of the century.[50] In general, throughout the course of the Weimar Republic, much of the program of the radical feminists was adopted by the Social Democratic Women's Movement.

NOTES

1. For studies emphasizing the changing character of the SPD, see Richard Hunt, *German Social Democracy, 1918-1933* (New Haven, 1964); Arthur Rosenberg, *Geschichte der Weimarer Republik* (Frankfurt/M, 1961); Carl Schorske, *German Social Democracy, 1905-1917: The Development of the Great Schism* (Cambridge, Massachusetts, 1955).

2. Anna Blos, *Die Frauenfrage im Lichte des Sozialismus* (Dresden, 1930), p. 95.

3. For an example of the war fever that infected Social Democrats, see Lily Braun, *Die Frauen und der Krieg* (Leipzig, 1915), pp. 8-9: "Those first August days were days which no one could forget if he lived to be 100. The entire population of Berlin lived in the streets; they no longer had homes: they felt only one fatherland, they had no families: only one people . . . the war destroyed the sentimental pacifism of women, their ridiculous dream of the sisterhood of all women." Or see the statement of Konrad Haenisch, an SPD Reichstag deputy, who wrote of his feelings those August days: "The battle of two souls in one breast was not easy for any of us . . . suddenly the terrible strain was dissolved, and one dared to be what one was—despite all torpid principles and wooden theories— for the first time [for the first time in a quarter-century!] to sing along with full heart, good conscience, and without fear of being thereby a traitor, in the rushing storm of song: *Deutschland, Deutschland über alles!*" Quoted in Eugen Prager, *Geschichte der USPD* (Berlin, 1921), p. 34. See also Joseph Berlau, *The German Social Democratic Party, 1914-1921* [New York, 1949).

4. *Gleichheit* (August 5, 1914), p. 337.

5. *Gleichheit* (September 4, 1914), p. 375.

6. Ibid., p. 374. For an example of the intellectual view of the war that Zetkin was refuting, see Thomas Mann, *Betrachtungen Eines Unpolitischen* (many editions).

7. Luise Dornemann, *Clara Zetkin* (Berlin, 1957), p. 226.

8. *Gleichheit* (January 5, 1915), p. 41.

9. *Gleichheit* did have a *feuilleton* section that featured serialized fiction on the plight of working-class girls or women.

10. *Gleichheit* (June 7, 1917), p. 117.

11. *Gleichheit* (August 17, 1917), p. 157.

12. Clara Zetkin, "Referat auf dem Vereinigungsparteitag der USPD (Linke) mit der KPD" (December 7, 1920), quoted in Clara Zetkin, *Zur Theorie und Taktik der kommunistischen Bewegung* (Leipzig, 1974), p. 429.

13. Clara Zetkin, "Was die Frauen Lenin Verdanken," quoted in Clara Zetkin, *Ausgewählte Reden und Schriften* (Berlin, 1960), 3: 163.

14. Clara Zetkin, "Begrüssungsrede auf dem XIII Parteitag der kommunistischen Partei Russlands" (May 23, 1924), quoted in Zetkin, *Ausgewählte Reden*, 3: 4.

15. Robert Wheeler, "German Women and the Communist International: The Case of the Independent Social Democrats," *Central European History*, no. 2 (June, 1975), pp. 113-139.

16. Clara Zetkin, *Die Internationale, Zeitschrift für Praxis und Theorie des Marxismus, 1919* 2/3: 15-20, and July 12, 1925, pp. 57-59. Reproduced in Institut für Marxistische Studien und Forschungen, ed., *Arbeiterbewegung und Frauenemanzipation, 1889-1933* (Frankfurt/M, 1973), pp. 42-71.

17. Clara Zetkin, "Warum brauchen wir Kommunisten eine Frauenbewegung," *Die Kommunistin* 14 (1919): 17-18, and 15 (1919): 116-117, reproduced in *Arbeiterbewegung und Frauenemanzipation*, 1889-1933, pp. 36-42.

18. For the mixed feelings of Social Democratic women on the contribution of Clara Zetkin, see Marie Juchacz, *Sie lebten für eine bessere Welt* (Berlin-Hannover, 1955), pp. 42-44; and Anna Blos, *Sozialismus und Frauenfrage*, pp. 24-25.

19. Fritzmichael Roehl, *Marie Juchacz und die Arbeiterwohlfahrt* (Hannover, 1961), p. 16. It may be revealing of Juchacz, or Roehl, or the 1950s, when the biography was written, or all three, that Roehl never mentions Juchacz's feminist activities.

20. Ibid., p. 26.

21. Ibid., p. 52.

22. Werner Thoennessen, *Frauenemanzipation. Politik und Literatur der Deutschen Sozialdemokratie* (Frankfurt/M, 1969), p. 131.

23. Quoted in Roehl, *Marie Juchacz*, p. 110.

24. Juchacz, *Sie lebten für eine bessere Welt*, p. 11.

25. Ibid.

26. Ibid., p. 47.

27. Ibid., pp. 48-55.

28. Ibid., p. 11.

29. *Gleichheit* (September 4, 1914), p. 110.

30. Luise Zietz, *Die Sozialdemokratischen Frauen und der Krieg* (Stuttgart, 1915).

31. *Stenographische Berichte über die Verhandlungen des Reichstags*, 361: 13657 (hereafter cited as *Sten. Berichte*).

32. Blos, *Die Frauenfrage*, p. 87.

33. See Chapter 3 of this book.

34. Blos, *Die Frauenfrage*, p. 109.

35. *Sten. Berichte*, 361: 12539. The German text reads: "Schlechterdings unmöglich sollte es in unserem Vaterlande, bei unserem männlichen Volke sein, dass Staatsbeamte höheren oder niederen Grades, mögen es nun Oberlehrer oder Briefträger sein, einer Frau gehorchen."

36. The text of the letter sent to the German chancellor read: "Im Interesse des Völkerfriedens der Zukunft, im Interesse des inneren Friedens des deutschen Volkes, im Interesse der Kultur, der Freiheit und des Fortschritts verlangen die deutschen Frauen die volle politische Gleichberechtigung mit dem Manne. [Signed] Die sozialdemokratischen Frauen Deutsch-

lands: Marie Juchacz. Die Frauen der Fortschrittlichen Volkspartei: Helene Lange. Die Frauen der Nationalliberalen Partei: Klara Mende. Das Arbeiterinnensekretariat der Generalkommission der Freien Gewerkschaften: Gertrud Hanna. Der Deutsche Frauenausschuss für dauernden Frieden: Lida Gustava Heymann. Der deutsche Reichsverband für Frauenstimmrechtsbund: Anita Augspurg. Der Bund Deutscher Frauenvereine: Dr. Gertrud Bauemer." *Gleichheit* (October 25, 1918), p. 25.

37. "Aufruf des Rates der Volksbeauftragten an das Deutsche Volk" (November 12, 1918), in Ernst Rudolf Huber, *Dokumente zur Deutschen Verfassungsgeschichte*, (Mainz, 1966), 3: 6-7.

38. Fifty-four percent of German women and 46 percent of German men were eligible to vote in 1919. The percentage of all women voting was 82.3 percent; the percentage of all men voting was 82.4 percent.

39. Thoennessen, *Frauenemanzipation*, p. 131.

40. *Frauenstimmen aus der Nationalversammlung* (Berlin, 1920). All contributors were members of the SPD.

41. Johanna Tesch, "Rückblick aus Ausblick," *Frauenstimmen aus der Nationalversammlung*, pp. 79-80.

42. *Sten. Berichte*, 326: 177-181.

43. Ibid.

44. Ibid., p. 233.

45. Huber, *Dokumente*, pp. 45-47.

46. Mathilde Wurm, *Reichstag und Frauenrechte* (Berlin, 1924), p. 2.

47. Ibid., p. 3.

48. Johanna Reitze, "Sollen die Frauen eigene Wege gehen," *Frauenstimmen*, pp. 15-17.

49. Marie Juchacz, "Die Frau als Staatsbürgerin," *Frauenstimmen*, p. 14.

50. Richard Evans, *The Feminist Movement in Germany, 1894-1933* (London, 1976).

3

WOMEN AS POLITICIANS: ORGANIZING FOR EQUALITY

THE TASK OF German women in the 1920s was to make their newly won constitutional equality tangible. While the revolutionary left continued to call for the overthrow of bourgeois society as the only way to emancipate women and the bourgeois women's movement became conservative, with many feminists becoming attracted to *völkisch* and protofascist ideas,[1] Social Democratic women remained a progressive force in German society. They struggled with the question of what equality for women meant, fought for social legislation that would ease the life of the working-class woman and mother, and attempted to educate women politically and bring them into the Social Democratic Party.

PROBLEMS OF IDEOLOGY: THE QUESTION OF EQUALITY

What equality for women means remains one of the more significant questions of the struggle for women to change their subordinate social and sexual status. This continued to be one of the troubling questions within German Social Democracy. No one in the party believed that obtaining the vote and securing certain constitutional rights constituted equality for women. Social Democrats, however, were unable to define very well what emancipation for women meant or how it was to be achieved.

In his study of the SPD and women's emancipation, the Frankfurt sociologist Werner Thoennessen stressed that the struggle for equality within the SPD was lost when the SPD abandoned revolutionary socialism. By abandoning revolutionary socialism, the SPD also abandoned the socialist theory of women's emancipation. Thoennessen has also suggested that when the SPD abandoned the socialist theory of women's emancipation, it returned to a traditional view of women.[2]

Thoennessen's evidence for the abandonment of the socialist theory of women's emancipation consisted of a series of articles by Edmund Fischer in the revisionist SPD journal, *Sozialistische Monatshefte*. In 1905 and again in 1917, Fischer maintained that women belonged in the home and that emancipation was contrary to women's nature and human nature and consequently unrealizable. Thoennessen believed that though the SPD never officially endorsed Fischer's views, the majority of its members must have shared them. He supported this thesis, noting that the SPD did very little to promote the cause of women's emancipation in the 1920s.

Although it is true that the abandonment of revolutionary socialism and the loss of Clara Zetkin changed the women's movement, there was more to the socialist analysis of women's oppression than its solution through revolutionary action. The socialist analysis of women's oppression continued to shape the thinking of Social Democratic women and was responsible for the focus on economic oppression during the Weimar Republic. Furthermore, there is little evidence to support the view that a socialist revolution in 1918 would have brought women any closer to equality than did the establishment of parliamentary democracy in Germany. A case in point was the observations of a woman participant in the November Revolution, who wrote:

> The mass of women played no role in the November days, because it was still taken for granted that men made politics . . . with few exceptions there were no women in the soldiers and workers councils. . . . At the first general congress of the workers and soldiers councils there were two women delegates [out of 490].[3]

The Weimar Republic did not witness the liberation of women, but there was some progress, probably as much as or more than

in any other nation. It was the Social Democrats who took the
lead in promoting progressive legislation in the areas of abortion and marriage and divorce reform. This legislation did not
endorse traditional views of women but sought to give them
more control over their lives. No doubt, many Social Democrats shared Fischer's views, but party policy and certainly the
female leadership recognized that the conditions of life in industrial society required that women work as wage laborers.
There is no evidence to suggest that any political Social Democratic woman longed for or thought a return to the home was
a realistic solution. Social Democratic women never abandoned
the socialist theory of women's emancipation, even if they abandoned Clara Zetkin and revolution. While they no longer could
draw upon the work of Clara Zetkin, now the outspoken member
of an opposition party, they had no problems paying homage
to August Bebel. Throughout the 1920s, they continued to view
Bebel's *Woman under Socialism* as the definitive work on the
woman question.[4]

The evidence seems to suggest that rather than abandoning
socialist ideas, the Social Democratic Women's Movement in the
1920s showed the limitations of the socialist interpretation of
woman's plight as articulated by Bebel and Zetkin. Their failure
lay not in their abandonment of socialist theory but in their
hesitation to go beyond it. Socialist theory, while it raised the
problem of women's oppression, did not solve it theoretically.[5]
Although socialist theory recognized that the oppression of
women preceded capitalism, it did not draw the logical conclusion
that the oppression of women in patriarchal *and* capitalist society
was economic and psychosexual. Capitalism profited from the
segmentation of society and the oppression of women, but it
did not create it. The oppression of women has been intrinsic
to patriarchal societies, in which men, women, culture, and
reality itself are male-defined and where women are viewed as
being different or, in Simone de Beauvoir's words, as "the Other."
Socialist theory is useful for understanding the particular nature
of the oppression of women under capitalism; however, it had
not been useful for understanding their oppression per se.[6] The
classic socialist theory was inadequate, and Social Democratic

women were hindered in their work and their vision not because they abandoned it but more because they confined themselves to it.

Socialist theory did help Marie Juchacz and other Social Democratic women understand that the vote and constitutional equality were not very meaningful in assuring equality for women. They were very much in the socialist tradition when they continually emphasized that political/legalistic equality was meaningless without economic equality. They worked to bring about this economic equality by sponsoring legislation and by educating women to become a political force and to fight for their economic self-interest. Their analysis of society was based on a division of society according to class rather than sex. Consequently, they failed to build solidarity and consciousness among women as women oppressed and exploited economically, psychologically, and sexually and were unable to rise to new levels of understanding of the condition of women in modern society.

A reconceptualization might have eventually evolved out of the Social Democratic Women's Movement had the movement not been destroyed by the advent of fascism in 1933. By the 1930s, isolated voices within the movement spoke for the need to go beyond the old socialist analysis. Metta Corssen, a regular contributor to *Sozialistische Monatshefte*, wrote in 1927:

A peculiar situation arose when the equality achieved through suffrage made the bourgeois women's movement problematic. Within the proletariat, however, the consequence of this equality meant the actual beginning of a real women's movement; the beginning of the struggle for that place next to man. It remains to be seen if out of this struggle socialist women will develop their own theory of women's emancipation.[7]

Socialist women did not develop their own theory, but a few isolated voices touched upon the problem by questioning the role and position of women in the family. As head of an organization and as a party functionary, Marie Juchacz was hesitant to deal with this issue head on, although it must have been obvious to her, having escaped an unhappy marriage, that women's family role presented a major obstacle to their integration into political and social life.[8]

At the 1925 party congress in Heidelberg, a delegate from Berlin expressed the problem that plagued politically active women:

> I believe not a single woman active in public life has been spared the question: how does your family feel about your work? Such a question is never asked of a man. The opinion of our comrades is that the family precedes our work in public life. We must fight this attitude and give women equality. . . . We must free ourselves from the old view that woman belongs in the house.[9]

Clara Bohm-Schuch, another Social Democratic activist, charged that all too often one heard men in the party say, "Thank God, I don't have a political wife."[10] Tony Pfuelf, a teacher, parliamentary delegate, and long-time party activist, insisted that the proletariat male differed little from his bourgeois counterpart in his concept of women as property and that the life of the party depended upon dealing with this question. The party, she charged, was not clearly committed in its program to the goal of the development of women to self-conscious, independent human beings.[11]

After a decade of organizational work and an ever-increasing female membership, Anna Geyer suggested a new women's program for the party congress to be held at Magdeburg in 1929. It was to include housework as the responsibility of both husband and wife, motherhood as a service women performed for society, and child rearing as the responsibility of the community, not the individual. Geyer correctly believed that her proposals were too radical to receive the support of most men or most women.[12]

The Magdeburg congress was especially significant for SPD women because women's issues were to be discussed at the regular party meeting rather than, as was the normal practice, at a special and succeeding women's congress. The closest the Magdeburg congress came to dealing with the issues suggested by Anna Geyer was the suggestion of a woman delegate that the SPD must begin addressing the personal experiences of women and not rely upon the socialist analyses of Engels and Bebel for an analysis of women's oppression. She also warned that the SPD must not use women merely to get votes for the party but must raise them up as equal members in the political struggle.[13] The Magdeburg congress, however, dismissed Geyer's proposals and continued to focus on the economic question of women's right to work and the old analysis that women's plight in the family was a result not of biological or sexual dependency but purely an outcome of their subordinate economic status.[14]

While the SPD officially continued to stress women's economic dependence, under the influence of the psychologist Alfred Adler, new psychological analyses were appearing to support the views of women such as Anna Geyer. Two such works, both by Social Democrats, were *Die Sozialisierung der Frau*, 1922 *(The Socialization of Women)* and *Die Frau unter dem Kapitalismus*, 1932 *(Women under Capitalism)*. These works had no impact on official SPD policy, but they—like Anna Geyer, Metta Corssen, and Tony Pfuelf—are of interest in suggesting that a new analysis might eventually have come out of the Social Democratic Women's Movement. In *The Socialization of Woman*, Otto Ruehle wrote that the advent of socialism meant a revolution in marital, sexual, and reproductive life. His wife, Alice Ruehle-Gerstel, greatly elaborated on this in *Woman under Capitalism*, which illuminated the problem of political women working under the handicap of male-defined identities.

> Socialist women of all persuasions have shown themselves to be as truly feminine as their bourgeois counterparts. They follow their men to elections, strikes, and demonstrations as the latter follow their men into war. . . . The working-class movement is despite its nonsexist [*geschlechtsindifferent*] program still a male affair. The women's groups of the Social Democratic and Communist Parties are not able to eliminate the sexual differences which rule the party. They work at secondary tasks at the request of and usually under the direction of men. Even in the revolutionary organization of the proletariat, true emancipation cannot be achieved.[15]

Marie Juchacz, while sometimes chiding men for their attitudes
toward women in the party, preferred not to stress this problem.
Instead, she preferred to emphasize organization and the achievement of economic equality. Juchacz, like Zetkin, did not want
to emphasize the struggle of women against men but to struggle
with men for the creation of a better society. At the Magdeburg
congress of 1929, she gave a report on women in politics and the
economy. The determining factor of the woman question is and
was the economic condition of women, Juchacz told her audience.
As the authorities on the subject, she referred to Bebel's *Woman
under Socialism* and Lily Braun's *Frauenfrage*, as well as the prewar *Gleichheit* and *Vorwärts*.[16]

In dealing with the question of women's emancipation, she
said that the SPD had to come to grips with the reality of an
increasing number of women working outside the home while
they continued to be mothers. The entrance of women into the
labor force was difficult as long as they continued to be mothers.

Juchacz also dealt with the general hostility toward women
working outside the home, which by 1929 was expressing itself
vehemently in the popular press: "The right of woman to work
for wages and especially that of the married woman is not a
controversy in the leadership of the party and the working-class
movement."[17]

Of course, there was some hostility in the working-class movement toward women working outside the home, but the SPD
held to its program and supported women's right to work even
under the pressure of increasing unemployment. It was up to
Marie Juchacz to explain to working-class men that they had
nothing to fear from women. She did this by supporting the
traditional division of labor, pointing out that in the industrial
labor force, with its clear division of male and female work, there
was not competition between men and women for jobs. If there
was competition for jobs in the industrial sector, it was a competition between women. The employment of women was a
more significant issue for the middle class, she explained, where
a few women were competing with men for dwindling professional jobs. She also pointed out that the question of women's
right to work for wages was rather absurd in an economy in

which by 1925 one-third of the female population, or 11,477,000
women, was employed.

Women had a right to work, and they had a right to be protected as mothers. It was a serious contradiction of capitalism
that women worked at jobs that took them away from home
for long hours every day and continued to be mothers. Consequently, the primary responsibility of a socialist party was to
protect women's rights as workers and as mothers. As a wage
laborer, woman suffered from the fact that she was a second-
class citizen subject to discrimination in economic and social
life. All women suffered from discrimination, but it was the
woman who worked for wages, struggling for her very existence,
who felt this discrimination most profoundly. In addition to suffering as a wage laborer, she suffered in the fulfillment of "her
highest calling—motherhood" because of the ethical and social
presumptions of bourgeois society.[18]

The recognition of the woman as wage laborer and as mother
was the motivating consciousness behind the work of Marie
Juchacz and the social legislation introduced by the SPD in the
Weimar Republic. In the transition to socialism, the role of a
political party was to ameliorate this contradiction between
the woman as wage laborer and as mother, as much as possible.
Marie Juchacz's work was hindered by having to work within
a parliamentary system where it was not in the interest of political parties to understand this contradiction.

ORGANIZATION

As part of a political party that had committed itself to working within the framework of parliamentary democracy toward a
gradual evolution to socialism, Marie Juchacz had to gauge her
work in terms of number of votes and members won to the party.
By the late 1920s, she was optimistic that progress was being
made and could point with some success to her work. Even in a
retrospective analysis written in the 1950s, she thought that the
SPD women's movement had been making definite progress that
had been halted only by an outside force—fascism.[19]

If success is gauged by numbers, then Marie Juchacz could
conclude that she was addressing herself to the proper issues

and taking the proper actions to advance the participation of women in Weimar politics. The women's movement, which had hit a low point at the time of the inflation in 1923, grew after the stabilization to over 230,000 members by 1931, or 22.8 percent of the total party membership.[20]

Despite her initial assurance that the women's movement would be integrated into the party, Juchacz, like Zetkin, continued to maintain a separate women's division within the party. Because political equality had not solved the woman question, she reasoned that special care and attention had to be paid to win women to the party and to socialism.[21] She emphasized continually the organization of women at the grass roots level and encouraged women to gain political experience in local politics. In Weimar, a larger percentage of women were politically active on the national level than on the state and community levels. Juchacz deplored the fact that there was such a variation in party membership on the local level. By 1925, some areas had a female membership of 27.6 percent, while others had only 5.8 percent.[22] Berlin always had a high percentage of politically active women, while in the small towns and hamlets of Germany, women more tied to their traditional role had a much more difficult time becoming actively involved in the political life of the communities. At the national level, in the Reichstag, women made up 10 percent or more of the SPD delegates. On the local level, in city governments, on the other hand, they made up only 4 percent of public officials, while in the rural villages the percentage was negligible.[23] It was on the communal level that Juchacz felt sexist attitudes[24] continued to persist most strongly to the detriment of women's political involvement. She suggested that women be more assertive in gaining positions of power and influence. Juchacz herself, however, took pride in the fact that she was not aggressive or "pushy" about promoting her own career.

As before 1914, the women's movement of the Weimar Republic continued to stress the importance of political education, and women's reading groups continued to discuss Marx, Engels, and Bebel. In 1931, Marie Juchacz reported that the party's educational efforts with women centered around giving women a socialist theoretical basis for the discussion of

political and economic questions. Local groups reported that
discussions centering around socialist theory were especially
popular.[25]

Marie Juchacz continued to approach women on an intellectual level and to educate them in politics and economics;
however, she increasingly came to believe that the best way
to educate women to socialism was not through theory but
through practical work. Consequently, after 1922, a major
part of her energies and efforts was directed toward involving
women in the work of the *Arbeiterwohlfahrt.* Through practical
social welfare work, work that would be more congenial to the
politically uninitiated, she believed that she could involve wom-
en in the work of the party and win them to the cause of socialism. Again and again, she insisted that the growing membership of women in the party was due to the recruitment and raising of political consciousness through work in the *Arbeiterwohlfahrt.*

The attitude of the party itself toward expending money and
energy to win women to the party was rather ambivalent. Even
though the party appreciated the significance of the woman
voter and was theoretically committed to equality for women,
it left the wooing and winning of women up to the women's
movement. The party did not discuss women's issues except
through the existence of the women's movement. It believed
that it had done its part in giving women the vote and now
expected some gratitude and appreciation. Marie Juchacz and
the women's movement were always on the defensive when,
after every election, it was shown that women did not overwhelmingly favor the SPD with their votes.

Within the party, men did not see a need to promote women
for positions of influence and power except in conjunction with
the women's movement. There was strong competition for such
positions, and men were not interested in adding another element
to this competition. Clara Bohm-Schuch explained that competition for positions within the party had emerged after such positions had become remunerative.[26]

The fact that there seemed to be no significant political benefits to be gained by promoting the equality of women hurt the
women's cause in Weimar and accounts for the lack of interest

of the SPD in women's issues. It was a great disappointment to
the SPD that women failed to vote for the party that had given
them a voice. In 1919, the party made a great effort to win the
women's vote. That year, it published twelve special pamphlets
dealing with women's concerns. Also, an expanded *Gleichheit*
was to appear weekly, featuring the addition of a section entitled "The Woman and Her House." That year, the party also
had 48 women delegates out of a total of 415 at its congress.
This was the high point of efforts on behalf of women.

After 1919, the general feeling was that the women's vote
had not helped, but hindered, the party. The question existed
in the minds of many party functionaries of whether the wom-
en's vote had not aided conservative forces and retarded progress.[27] In 1928, Anna Siemsen wrote that, in general, the belief
in Germany was that the women's vote had had reactionary consequences.[28] Analyses of the 1950s also maintained that the
women's vote in Germany was a conservative rather than a progressive force.[29]

There were a variety of explanations for this phenomenon
among Social Democrats. Some suggested that women were
politically naive, more easily swayed by the most popular party
in the district and more subject to direct political pressure.[30]
Others have suggested that the more sensitive nature of women
was offended by the controversy among socialists that had resulted in the formation of three socialist parties.[31] The most
common view was that women tended to be more religious and
therefore repelled by the non-Christian socialists. The statistical
evidence, while not completely persuasive, tends to bear out this
latter view. The party that seemed to gain most from the women's
vote was the Center Catholic Party.[32] A United Nations-sponsored
study of voting behavior of women in Germany lent great importance to the religious factor in explaining the voting behavior of
Weimar women. The author noted that, as early as 1922, *Gleichheit*, recognizing the importance of religion to women, suggested
to campaign workers that they take care to spare religious feelings.[33]

Whatever the reason for women's lack of interest in expressing
their gratitude to the SPD, the party in the 1920s showed a de-

creasing interest in courting women. This became especially marked after 1925, despite the fact that membership of women in the party was increasing. Winning the women's vote was delegated to the women's movement, which was given the responsibility of "delivering" the women's vote[34] and criticized when it failed.

In general, men tended to stay out of women's issues and women tended to concentrate on them. Men addressed themselves to these issues only when they concerned money, loss of membership, and lack of women's votes. Generally, women's issues were relegated to the women's conferences that followed the regular party meetings. This fact probably also hindered the development and discussion of concerns important to women. An attempt was made in 1925 to hold the women's conferences before the regular party meeting in order to bring well-formulated women's issues to the general party congress. This move, however, was met with scorn and derision by the men. "We do not care to hatch the eggs laid by the women," was the comment of one male delegate. The women were told that the party would formulate the guidelines for the women's meetings and that women were to carry out the program of the party, and not vice versa.[35]

Women's conferences, under the direction of Marie Juchacz, were held after the party congresses in 1919, 1921, 1924, and 1927. Their aim was to discuss those issues of particular concern to women. The issues discussed dealt with everything from the women's movement to housing, abortion, discriminatory laws, the women's journals, protection for mothers, and temperance. Women also used these occasions to express their anger and frustration at the lack of understanding and chauvinism of their male comrades within the party.

The first postwar women's conference, guided by Marie Juchacz, stressed the solidarity and loyalty of women to the party as a whole. This was important, considering that the women's movement under Clara Zetkin had caused some distress for the majority Social Democrats. Though women had special interests, these interests could best be served within the framework of the party organization, Juchacz told her audience. She also urged women to participate in all aspects of party work and optimistically believed that it would be only a matter of time until there would be a significant number of politically experienced women who could play an active role in the party.[36]

Juchacz stressed that equality had not been won with the vote and that women could hardly afford to sit back and enjoy the gains made: "We women must press forward to full economic and personal freedom. That is possible only through socialism."[37] Juchacz further noted that the revolution had done nothing to destroy the psychological differences between the sexes and that women continued to have interests that men could not understand or for which they showed little concern.[38] She did not note that the aims of the party and women's interests were not necessarily always compatible.

Already, at this first conference, SPD women were reprimanded by one of their male comrades, who chided them that the women's vote had been a reactionary force. The successes of the Center and German National People's Parties (*Deutsch Nationale Volkspartei*) were clearly due to the women's vote, they were told.[39]

In 1921, at Goerlitz, there appeared the first signs of pessimism and discouragement after the gains of 1919. Juchacz complained that women had allowed themselves to be pushed into the background again and appeared only as tokens on committees and delegations.[40] Nevertheless, the 1921 congress reaffirmed its commitment to women and included in its program "the struggle for total constitutional and actual equality for all citizens without regard to origin, religion, or sex, and equal education for both sexes by both sexes."[41] The program also advocated protective legislation calling for restrictions on night work for women, on work with dangerous machines, and work that was especially damaging to health. Above all, the party program stressed the right of women to work for wages.[42]

There was no women's conference for three years after Goerlitz. When the next one was held, in 1924 in Berlin, women were still on the defensive, being told that women's suffrage seemed to be the major obstacle in the progress toward socialism.[43] In addition, women were admonished that the purpose of the women's conferences was to strengthen the effectiveness of the SPD.[44] In its organization statute of that year, the party conceded to the women's movement the demand that in the leadership of all organizations and all delegations, women were to be represented in relationship to their total membership.[45]

At Heidelberg in 1925, the SPD formulated a new program, which reaffirmed the party's Marxist ideology and again proclaimed women's equal right to work and the right to equal education. It also demanded the equality of women in the civil code and divorce reform.[46] Despite repeated attempts, the SPD had little success in changing the civil code, a relic of Wilhelminian society, which discriminated against women and was often in contradiction to the constitution. The Weimar political system did not provide for a challenge to the civil code on the basis of its constitutionality or unconstitutionality. Consequently, in Weimar, Germans lived with the contradictions of a progressive constitution and a conservative civil code.

The last of the women's conferences was held in Kiel in 1927. Germany had recovered from the inflation and was prospering. Consequently, a feeling of optimism pervaded that conference, and Marie Juchacz was able to report: "Women in increasing number are entering political life, as well as the economic and administrative system of the state. We note how, slowly but surely, women are rising into full citizen status."[47]

She continued to be optimistic that all was going well with the women's movement when, two years later, the party met at Magdeburg. Membership was continuing to grow and had almost reached its prewar level. The main event for women at the Magdeburg congress was Juchacz's previously discussed report on the state of women in politics and the economy.

The 1931 party congress at Leipzig had no special discussion of women. After 1930, Social Democratic women were increasingly concerned with the National Socialist danger and its misogynistic ideology. "In first place was the fight against National Socialism," Juchacz reported in the 1931 yearbook. Social Democratic women sponsored courses, lectures, and slide shows to alert women to the danger. *Genossin*, the journal of SPD women functionaries, was filled with analyses of National Socialism and women's rights. In 1933, the worst fears of the Social Democratic Women's Movement came true when the National Socialists seized power and the reactionary view of women as best serving society by service in the home and within the family prevailed.[48]

"Politically conscious women did not have enough time to introduce women to their new responsibilities," Marie Juchacz wrote after the war in *Sie lebten für eine bessere Welt*, her biographical sketches of socialist women. After 1933, the discussion of the political role of women ceased. Marie Juchacz herself, together with the entire executive committee of the SPD, was forced to flee Germany. Many of the other women leaders went underground. Juchacz's personal papers are filled with examples of the fate that befell politically active socialist women after 1933. The courageous Tony Pfuelf, who had fought for women's rights and educational opportunities in the parliament and who had protested the patronizing attitude of men at many party meetings, committed suicide in 1933. Gertrud Hannah, the leader of the women's trade union movement, committed suicide in 1944. Luise Kautsky died in Auschwitz. Many other known Social Democratic women were harassed, humiliated, and assaulted by Nazi thugs.[49]

THE SOCIAL DEMOCRATIC WOMEN'S JOURNALS

As a major instrument of the women's movement, the women's journals provide an enlightening example of the consciousness and direction of the party. *Gleichheit*, the original socialist women's journal, with its heavy theoretical and political tone under the editorship of Clara Zetkin, changed under its new editors Juchacz and later Clara Bohm-Schuch to be more appealing to a wider audience of working-class women. In 1919, *Gleichheit*, in imitation of popular bourgeois fashion magazines, added a bimonthly feature entitled "The Woman and Her House," which featured simple but stylish clothes for the working-class woman.

Gleichheit, its new editor announced in 1919, had to deal with practical problems and become comprehensible to the majority of working-class women. Its traditional format had been too political and theoretical to interest the majority.[50] Although the radical tone of *Gleichheit* had been objectionable to party leaders for a long time, its new format did not bring their enthusiastic support. After the war, the party leadership was increasingly unwilling to support the journal financially. Finally, in 1923, during the height of the inflation, the organ of the women's movement for 32 years ceased publication.

Gleichheit was succeeded in 1924 by *Frauenwelt (Woman's World)*, which was similar in style to bourgeois women's magazines but with a socialist message. *Frauenwelt*, published from 1924 to 1933, was edited by a man, Dr. Lohmann. It was a colorful magazine featuring fashions, household hints, art, and short stories with a socialist moral. Its aim was to make socialist ideals appealing to women. Though its articles were not political in the traditional sense of the word, some dealt with issues of great significance for women. There were articles on sex and explicit discussions and instructions on different methods of birth control, as well as articles on the rights of married women in relationship to their husbands.[51] There were also articles on women who led nontraditional lives, such as the artist Kaethe Kollwitz, Rosa Luxemburg, and Marie Juchacz. A 1924 article that ascribed women's personal unhappiness in love and marriage to the unequal power relationship between men and women could even be described as radically feminist.[52]

Frauenwelt served a useful function, but it was not well received by women functionaries in the party, who considered it much too frivolous and completely inadequate for their purposes. Under their urging, the SPD eventually financed another publication for women functionaries, which was to deal with political and organizational questions. This publication, *Genossin*, began publication in 1924 and continued to exist throughout the Weimar Republic.

SOCIAL DEMOCRATIC WOMEN
IN THE REICHSTAG

In addition to the vote and work in party politics, Weimar
Germany gave women the first opportunity to participate in
the legislative process itself. Women made up 54 percent of the
voters in the Weimar Republic, but they never made up more
than 9.6 percent (in 1919) of the Reichstag delegates. After
1919, the number of women delegates averaged 7.2 percent.
This was discouragingly low, but nevertheless it was higher than
in most other Western countries.[53]

The participation of women in national politics was favored
by the proportional and list system of Weimar, where voters
voted for a list drawn up by parties and not for individuals. As
all parties were eager to court the women's vote, a few women
were always included on the list. This also meant, of course,
that women were particularly dependent upon the party for in-
clusion on the list.

As members of party delegations in a system that emphasized
party discipline, women as a group did not have much of a
chance of making a real impact in the Reichstag. Women of
all parties tended to promote social legislation, but as most of
the political parties of the Weimar Republic were committed to
ameliorating the harsh conditions of life through social legislation, such legislation would have been introduced even without
the presence of women.

Women never formed a women's caucus or coalition within
the Reichstag. They tended to vote with their parties rather
than with other women on issues. This was especially true in
legislation involving social-sexual relationships. Only occasionally
did women present a resolution together. Women of all parties,
for example, presented a resolution that would give women access
to law exams. Women also presented a united front in protesting
the firing of married women after World War I.

The division among women was most obvious when it came
to the "woman question." One scholar of the period, Claudia
Koonz, has explained that this was not necessarily due to the fact
that women were oblivious to the plight of women in German

society or that they were male-identified women who had little use for other women. All women in the Reichstag identified with women and worked for the equality of women, but there was sharp disagreement among women on what constituted equality. These disagreements tended to follow class lines.

Socialist women wanted to integrate women fully into Weimar society by acknowledging their rights as workers while taking into account women's special needs and problems as mothers. In practice, this meant that Social Democratic women worked for protective legislation for women workers and changes in family law.

Bourgeois women, Conservative, Catholic, and Liberal, also advocated women's equality but worked to increase women's power within their own traditional domain. They worked to protect the family. Claudia Koonz concluded:

> Thus women's perceptions of their own best interests varied according to their ideological commitments and life experiences. The socialists' faith in class solidarity conflicted with the nonsocialists' belief in family solidarity. Because of the extreme polarization of this issue, the Reichstag did not pass any reforms which might have weakened the patriarchal family structure. . . . Rhetorically all politicians agreed that women could become equal. Wives and mothers could not.[54]

The Social Democratic Party always had in its delegation the most women of any party. There was never any public disagreement between men and women on issues. This was in keeping with the practice of party discipline, which women as newcomers to the political process followed judiciously.

Marie Juchacz set the tone for female Reichstag delegates when she declared in her introductory speech that the political struggle of women could now be carried on within the framework of party politics.[55] Working in a once exclusively male area, women, however, would remain women. "It would not occur to us to deny our womanhood [*Frauentum*] just because we have stepped into the political arena,"[56] she declared. In practical terms, this meant that women should work in areas especially

suitable for them: the administration of widow and orphan welfare, aid for the wounded, education, social politics, protection
of mothers, housing, public health, youth, unemployment, and
the civil rights of women.

The only protest to Juchacz's designation of certain areas for
women came from longtime activist Luise Zietz, who was to be
one of the more visible women in the Reichstag, speaking to all
issues, not just those deemed suitable and proper for women.
Unfortunately, Zietz died in 1922.[57]

While women of all parties worked on issues of education,
social welfare, and population policies, Social Democratic wom-
en tackled issues that offended the bourgeois morality of their
Reichstag sisters. One such issue concerned the automatic firing
of unmarried female civil servants who became pregnant. Social
Democratic women considered this law inhumane and discriminatory (because male civil servants did not suffer the same penalties)
and brought the issue to a vote in the Reichstag, but they were
defeated, with all the women of the bourgeois parties voting
against them.[58]

Some of the favorite issues of SPD women were the improve-
ment of the legal situation of unmarried mothers and illegitimate
children, as well as the abolition of paragraph 218 of the civil
code, which made abortion a criminal offense. The struggle of
SPD women to ameliorate the harsh consequences of bourgeois
morality for women will be discussed in more detail in the next
chapter. In general, Social Democrats—men and women—were
prepared to take a much more progressive stance on moral and
sexual issues than bourgeois women.

The nature of party and parliamentary politics made it impossible for women to attain any real influence or power. In
the areas of foreign policy, finance, and all of the significant
issues that were to determine the fate of Germany, women were
excluded. Because of their sex, women were excluded from
patronage, from the smoke-filled rooms of the political salons.
In short, they were excluded from all of the behind-the-scenes
politicking so intrinsic to parliamentary politics and so essential
for attaining positions of power and influence within the system.
The role and significance of these political salons in Weimar as

the places where influence was traded and decisions made are only now beginning to emerge. No woman was ever invited to these salons, where Weimar ministers, party leaders, military leaders, and captains of industry met to make decisions in a congenial atmosphere of fat cigars and fine brandies.[59]

NOTES

1. Richard Evans, *The Feminist Movement in Germany, 1894-1933* (London, 1976), p. 273.

2. Werner Thoennessen, *Frauenemanzipation. Politik und Literatur der Deutschen Sozialdemokratie* (Frankfurt/M, 1969), pp. 108-119.

3. Martha Arendsee, "Die Novemberrevolution und die Frauen," *Einheit* 2 (1948): 915-923.

4. In her Magdeburg speech of 1929, Juchacz credits both Bebel and the prewar *Gleichheit* for her concepts. *Protokoll über die Verhandlungen des Parteitags* (hereafter cited as *Protokoll*). (1929), p. 220.

5. I owe these views to my reading of contemporary radical feminists such as Shulamith Firestone, *The Dialectic of Sex* (New York, 1970); Sheila Rowbotham, *Woman's Consciousness, Man's World* (Middlesex, England, 1973); and especially Juliet Mitchell, *Woman's Estate* (New York, 1971).

6. The idea that there is an alternative to oppressive patriarchal social organization has been suggested, among others, by the work of Robert Briffault, *The Mothers* (New York, 1927); Evelyn Reed, *Woman's Evolution* (New York, 1975); and Erich Fromm, *The Crisis of Psychoanalysis* (New York, 1970).

7. Metta Corssen, "Die Problematik der Frauenbewegung," *Sozialistische Monatshefte* 33 (1927): 816.

8. The personal histories of women involved in political struggle are very enlightening. For example, Marie Juchacz was divorced and never remarried. Gertrud Hannah, Hedwig Wachenheim, and Tony Pfuelf never married. Clara Zetkin had been widowed at an early age, and a later marriage ended in divorce. Rosa Luxemburg never married (except on paper). Lily Braun was married but had a rather untraditional marital relationship. Political and social involvement, then as now, threatens women's personal and marital happiness and tranquility and consequently requires great sacrifice.

9. *Protokoll* (1925), p. 168.

10. *Genossin* 2 (1926): 51.

11. *Gleichheit* (March, 1929), p. 331.

12. *Genossin* (March, 1929), pp. 87-88.

13. *Protokoll* (1929), p. 238.

14. Ibid., p. 242.

15. Alice Ruehle-Gerstel, *Die Frau unter dem Kapitalismus* (Leipzig, 1932), p. 142.

16. *Protokoll* (1929), p. 220.

17. Ibid., p. 12.

18. Ibid., p. 220.

19. Marie Juchacz, *Sie lebten für eine bessere Welt* (Berlin, 1955), p. 1.

20. Membership figures are taken from SPD records. Membership as a whole also grew, and the relative percentage of women grew only slightly.

21. Marie Juchacz, *Praktische Winke für die Sozialdemokratische Frauenbewegung* (Berlin, 1919; reprint ed., Berlin, 1921), p. 4.

22. *Protokoll* (1925), p. 333.

23. *Genossin* (March, 1927), p. 69.

24. The word "sexism" is, of course, a modern term and concept. Social Democratic women had no such useful term to describe their experiences.

25. *Jahrbuch* (1931), p. 122.

26. *Genossin* 7 (1926): 208-209.

27. *Protokoll* (1919), pp. 523-531.

28. Anna Siemsen, "Die Frauenwahlen," *Sozialistische Monatshefte* 34 (1928): 573.

29. Gabrielle Bremme, *Die politische Rolle der Frau in Deutschland* (Goettingen, 1956), pp. 71-73; and Maurice Duverger, *The Political Role of Women* (UNESCO, 1955), pp. 50-67.

30. Siemsen, "Die Frauenwahlen," p. 578.

31. Max Schneider, "Die Deutsche Wählerin," *Die Gesellschaft* 2 (1927): 369.

32. The reliability of the statistical evidence is questionable. Separate voting of women and men took place only in some districts in Weimar and only at some elections. The most suggestive and extensive figures come from Cologne, which is a Catholic city and therefore may not be a reliable indicator for voting behavior in Germany as a whole.

33. Bremme, *Die politische Rolle der Frau*, p. 73.

34. One example of the party's declining interest in women can be found in *Sozialistische Monatshefte*, which published many articles on the woman question in the early 1920s. Gradually, the number of articles declined. By 1930, 1931, and 1932, there were no feature articles on women. After 1931, the regular column on the women's movement was discontinued.

35. *Protokoll* (1925), p. 185; (1927), p. 47.

36. *Protokoll* (1919), p. 249.

37. Ibid., p. 465.

38. Ibid., p. 461.

39. Ibid., p. 485.

40. *Protokoll* (1921), p. 11.

41. Ibid., pp. iv-vi.

42. Ibid., p. 223.

43. *Protokoll* (1924), p. 219.

44. Ibid., p. 5.

45. *Protokoll* (1925), pp. 8-9.

46. Ibid., p. 187.

47. *Protokoll* (1927), p. 380.

48. Jill Stephenson, *Women in Nazi Society* (New York, 1975). Stephenson writes that the rhetoric changed more than the reality of women's lives in the Third Reich. While Nazis talked of restricting women's work and sending women back into the home, the reality of German society required that women continue to work as wage laborers. This was especially true after the economy switched to war production and men were drafted.

49. Marie Juchacz Papers, *Nachlass* Vol. 4 (Friedrich Ebert Stiftung, Bonn).

50. *Protokoll* (1919), p. 467.

51. *Frauenwelt* (1924), pp. 177, 287; (1929), p. 441.

52. *Frauenwelt* (1929), p. 249.

53. Bremme, *Die politische Rolle der Frau,* and Claudia Koonz, "Conflicting Allegiances: Political Ideology and Women Legislators in Weimar Germany," *Signs* 1, part 1 (1976): 663-683.

54. Koonz, "Conflicting Allegiances," p. 683.

55. *Sten. Berichte,* 326: 177.

56. Ibid., pp. 177-181.

57. Ibid., p. 233.

58. Anna Blos, *Die Frauenfrage im Lichte des Sozialismus* (Dresden, 1930), p. 119.

59. This is according to a conversation with Dieter Buse in January, 1976. Buse is writing an article on the Hotzendorff salon and a biography of Friedrich Ebert, the first president of the Weimar Republic.

4

WOMEN AS WOMEN: FROM THE FAMILY TO SOCIETY— WOMEN'S TRADITIONAL ROLE REDEFINED

THE MOST SIGNIFICANT change that distinguished the postwar women's movement from the Zetkin era was the emphasis on social welfare work and social reforms to benefit women in their capacity as wives and mothers. This was not a change that occurred automatically and without discussion, but it fitted in well and naturally with a party now clearly reformist, committed to gradual evolutionary development toward socialism. It also provided the ideal synthesis of the socialist vision of women as socially productive and active and the bourgeois vision of the nurturing woman ministering to her family. The new Social Democratic woman would move from her traditional sphere in the family to carry out her traditional role in society as a whole. She would expand beyond the individual family to nurture and minister to the family of man.

MINISTERING TO SOCIETY: THE ARBEITERWOHLFAHRT AND WOMEN'S ROLE

Prior to World War I, social welfare work had been the province of bourgeois women, who had gradually professionalized it, raising it from the status of charity work done by Lady Bountifuls to work done by professionally trained women. During the war years, more and more working-class women became involved in social work, encouraged by the great human needs created by the war and by the organized Social Democratic Women's Movement. Even revolutionary socialists such as Clara Zetkin and Luise Zietz called upon their sisters to help bind the wounds of the bleeding social order.[1]

Once the war was over, however, the question of the appropriateness of socialists being involved in social welfare work was again raised in the Social Democratic movement. After all, socialists were to transform society, not alleviate the misery created by a decadent capitalism. The debate on this issue in 1919 centered around Marie Juchacz's desire to establish a working-class welfare organization to be known as the *Arbeiterwohlfahrt*.[2]

In addition to questioning the appropriateness of a working-class welfare organization from an ideological perspective, it was feared that the *Arbeiterwohlfahrt* would sap energy from the political movement and especially from the women's branch of that movement.[3] Thus Juchacz felt it necessary to justify the *Arbeiterwohlfahrt* in political terms: "When we give aid, we come politically closer to women. Women who are involved in public work are happy to have the opportunity to be able to work practically for other women. They mature politically."[4]

In finalizing her plans for the *Arbeiterwohlfahrt*, Juchacz reported that as early as 1913, she conceived of a working-class welfare organization run by working-class people themselves. At that time, she said, she realized that working-class women felt themselves degraded in accepting the charity of church or other bourgeois welfare organizations. As secretary of the SPD women's bureau in Cologne, she explored the possibility of organizing a self-help program with working-class women. Their first efforts centered around programs for children, organizing hikes out of the cities into the country for fresh air and sunshine.[5] It was difficult for anyone to raise political or ideological objections to this kind of program, and the later work of the *Arbeiterwohlfahrt* also continued to involve child welfare to a large extent.

During the war years, the energies of working-class women were absorbed by the already existing bourgeois welfare organizations. Once the war was over, however, working-class women

felt uncomfortable and no longer welcome in these organizations. Class bias had reasserted itself. Marie Juchacz, however,
was determined that working-class women should continue to
do the social welfare work begun in these years. At the national
assembly, she suggested, "Perhaps it will be shown . . . that the
strength of women lies in social politics and public welfare and
social work. Time will tell."[6] To fill the needs of working-class
people and to engage working-class women and men in efforts
to help themselves and others of their class, Juchacz then established the *Arbeiterwohlfahrt* in December, 1919. It was to be
a successful organization, which continues to exist in the Federal
Republic today.

The purpose of the organization, Juchacz wrote, was to carry
"the ideas of the working-class movement into social welfare
work . . . the idea of self-help, comradeship, solidarity, and the
idea that welfare must become a function of the state and its
institutions."[7] The *Arbeiterwohlfahrt* was to provide assistance
for all those who needed it without asking for political or religious affiliation. It was not to be in the tradition of other charita-
ble organizations, which, according to Juchacz, oppressed those
they aimed to assist. The *Arbeiterwohlfahrt* was to avoid the
charity syndrome and its accompanying baggage of the moral
superiority of those helping and the moral inferiority of those
being helped. It was to replace a demeaning and oppressive
charity with the socialist vision of an organized, self-conscious
working class aiding its weaker individual members while struggling to overthrow the system that made such aid necessary.

The *Arbeiterwohlfahrt* was also to serve as a way for working-
class women to gain entrance into the profession of social
work. It financially supported the studies of some working-
class women, persuaded schools of social work to lower entrance
requirements, and set up special short programs to make professional social work accessible to working-class women.

Both men and women participated in the work of the *Arbeiterwohlfahrt*, but the strongest participation was obviously by wom-
en. Marie Juchacz thought of the *Arbeiterwohlfahrt* as a bridge
between the private world of the home and family and the public
world of political action. Social work allowed women to step

out of the home but still work in areas related to traditional women's work.

By 1930, the *Arbeiterwohlfahrt* had 2,000 local organizations, and across Germany it provided many kinds of services: homes for teen-age girls, child care centers, soup kitchens, camps for children, care for pregnant women, and household help for ill and pregnant women as well as for those who had just had babies.

There was no discussion within the *Arbeiterwohlfahrt* of this kind of work perpetuating women's traditional role. Whatever feminist consciousness there was in the political women's movement, exemplified by women like Tony Pfuelf and others, did not carry over into welfare work. Typically the homes for teen-age girls run by the *Arbeiterwohlfahrt* perpetuated traditional bourgeois roles and attitudes. At these homes, girls learned how to run households, to sew, to embroider, to play music, and to garden.[8]

Juchacz considered the *Arbeiterwohlfahrt* to be limited. It was not to be an organization that could pretend to do away with even a small part of the general social misery.

> The leaders of the organization understand that other powers have to work on changing economic and social conditions. . . . The *Arbeiterwohlfahrt* . . . aims to help children and young people in their development, to support mature people in their struggle for existence, to give the old and invalid economic help and a little sunshine, and to educate those giving assistance to fulfill their duty in service to the community.[9]

WOMEN'S NEW SOCIAL ROLE: THE PAYOFF FOR WOMEN AND THE PARTY

The establishment of the *Arbeiterwohlfahrt* and the chance for women to become involved in social welfare work was opportune both for the party and for politically inexperienced women. Establishing a new parallel organization where women's energies and leadership could be channeled took the pressure off the party to provide meaningful work and positions for women within the party structure. Through the *Arbeiterwohlfahrt*, women could work for the goals of the party without threatening the party establishment in any way. The hypocrisy of the "separate but equal" spheres of influences was thereby established in the political working-class movement.

Enfranchising women and urging them to become involved in public life threatened to ameliorate some of the sharp distinctions between men's sphere and women's sphere. Although the politics of Social Democracy forced Social Democrats to be consistent in their logic and support widening women's sphere of influence from the home to the society at large, there was nothing in socialist ideology or theory that helped them cope with the threat to sexual distinctiveness posed by women entering the "men's world." The challenge to sex role distinctions was threatening to both men and women, and the psychological dilemma had to be resolved somehow. If women were now to be encouraged to become politically and socially involved, how should they behave? How should they relate to men? There were no models and no precedents for women entering public life in large numbers. The *Arbeiterwohlfahrt* and the emphasis on social work as the proper sphere for women in the world beyond the home provided a solution to the threat against sex roles and distinctions. With the establishment of social work as a legitimate area of activity for Social Democratic women, the differences between the sexes could be emphasized in public life as well as they had previously been emphasized by confining women to the home and family.

When this solution emerged, there was great relief and relaxation of tension in men and women, accompanied by an outpouring of sentimentality ascribing to women the most tender, humane, nurturing, life-giving and life-preserving qualities. The vision of woman as the savior of humanity followed the nineteenth-century bourgeois idealization of women and suggests that the working class was not prepared to transform bourgeois society but had already adopted some of its more contradictory values.

Articulating this solution in 1921 at the Goerlitz party congress was Frau Dr. Schoefer, a delegate: "Woman is the born guardian and protector of people; therefore, social work seems so appropriate for her."[10] Woman's place in political society was affirmed by her function as the protector of human life, she continued. As

males are suited for battle, females are suited to protect and pre-
serve life. As the male is more inclined to production, the female
is more inclined to deep involvement in human affairs. "Therefore, in the name of the community, women must be given the
task of protecting and preserving human life,"[11] she concluded.
For this new task for women Frau Dr. Schoefer invented a new
term: *Menschenoekonomie* (human economy). Human economy
involved primarily, but not exclusively, social work, and the
principle of human economy was to be carried over into all areas
of life, political and economic as well as social.[12] Frau Dr. Schoefer also defined the precise areas in which women were to concentrate their energies and efforts. She included women's rights
and the right to work as primary areas of work and thus
affirmed the long-standing primary goals and areas of struggle
for Social Democratic women. She stressed, however, that wom-
en were to concentrate on protection for mothers and working
women, child welfare, education, health, and care for the ill and
the weak and also to concern themselves with the problems of
alcoholism, venereal disease, and housing. Women were to be
the representatives of nurturing motherliness in all of these areas.
It was women's social duty to transform her "primitive" (biological) fertility to social fertility.[13] Frau Dr. Schoefer's speech
was greeted with enthusiastic applause and was accepted in a
summary form as a guideline by the women's conference.[14]

Men were only too happy to promote the notion of the humane, motherly qualities of women being transferred from
private to public life. One delegate proclaimed his delight with
women's involvement in social work in the following way: "It
was not right . . . that we [men] have had to work in areas
which lie far from the natural inclinations of men: charity,
youth welfare—areas for which the woman is born, but for which
men do not always have the proper understanding."[15]

Friedrich Stampfer paid tribute to women in writing that it
was woman's special task as citizen to humanize society through
her femininity (*Frauenart*) and to be political not in order to kill
but to heal. Women "are by nature determined to alleviate misery and heal wounds,"[16] he said. Paul Loebe, Reichstag president, recalled that the female delegates at the national assembly
were almost all properly feminine and motherly and gave his ap-

proval to the fact that most sought to work in areas suited to their feminine nature.[17]

The women's journals, *Frauenwelt* as well as *Gleichheit*, also portrayed the ideal woman as the self-sacrificing mother. The bourgeois ideal of the devoted, child-centered woman, which had emerged in the nineteenth century, had clearly permeated the working-class movement by the 1920s and was uncritically accepted by the political branch of the movement as the most ideal, if not in fact the only possible, model for women, replacing Bebel's model of the socialist woman of the future.

The acceptance of bourgeois values and the bourgeois ideal of womanhood was another example of the bourgeoisification of the German proletariat described by Richard Hunt in his study of the SPD in the 1920s. Bourgeoisification, Hunt explained, was inevitable, for by 1930, 35 percent of the leadership of the SPD came from middle-class backgrounds. In addition, "the interest of the proletarian cause required that functionaries adapt themselves to bourgeois forms and conventions."[18]

Among the rank and file, bourgeoisification was also an increasingly obvious phenomenon. Henrik de Man wrote in 1930: "The proletariat, even the class-conscious proletariat, is succumbing more and more to the inclination to imitate, in the unpolitical areas of daily living, the bourgeois or petty bourgeois style of life."[19] In another article, he observed: "The proletarian masses, who instinctively feel that cultural and social supremacy is a unity, are content with attempting to imitate the bourgeoisie, which they regard as a model of culture and good manners."[20]

Within the women's movement, there were some isolated criticisms of this trend. One woman complained in *Genossin* of the bourgeois life-style of SPD functionaries: "In our circles it is the first duty of woman to cultivate proletarian culture and a socialist life-style. . . . We are struggling not only for a new era but also for a new culture."[21]

Despite such isolated criticisms, the Social Democratic Women's Movement never dealt with the basic contradiction between the socially productive woman and the child- and family-centered woman. Its ideology continued to be based on the socialist theory that the key to women's emancipation was the involvement

by women in socially productive labor. On the other hand, it
promoted the bourgeois ideal of womanhood, which proclaimed
motherhood as woman's highest calling and the key to her self-
fulfillment. Included in this notion of womanhood were a devotion and attention to the task of mothering that were impossible
to combine with working outside the home for ten to twelve
hours a day. A woman's movement that failed to question and
confront the idealization of motherhood prevalent in modern
bourgeois society was bound to flounder on such contradictions.

Social Democratic women were not unique in having difficulty
in dealing with and resolving this contradiction; women politicians from the entire political spectrum, whether or not they
were mothers, all seemed determined to prove that public life
had not robbed them of their nurturing qualities. Regine Deutsch,
a contemporary political observer, summarized her analysis of
the work of women in the national assembly with the following
comments:

> Her most precious qualities, the ability to be loving and com-
> passionate, must remain unchanged. The love which the
> mother has up to now given her own children will not be
> diminished when she turns it to all children; the care which
> she has given to individuals, the public legislator will now
> give to all those who stand in the shadows of life. It has
> been clearly shown that the main interest—but not the only
> one—of women of all parties lies in this area. We recall the
> law for pregnancy assistance and welfare. Only women spoke
> for it . . . women of all parties were united in their concern
> for their sisters in their most dangerous hours . . . *they have
> all worked as social mothers*, from Frau Behm to Frau Zietz.[22]

This idealization of motherhood, which by the twentieth
century had permeated all social classes, was one of the most
characteristic aspects of bourgeois culture as it developed in
Europe in the eighteenth and nineteenth centuries. It emerged
as a reaction to the disintegration of the old traditional family
under the impact of industrialization and became the cornerstone for a new definition of family life and women's role with-

in it. Before industrialization undermined and destroyed the family's productive function, women as well as men had been economically productive members of the family. Their productive function was as significant as their reproductive function. Children were also productive members of the family. They were not the passive recipients of the mother's devotion and attention, a modern development related to women's loss of productivity in the family.

By the 1920s, Social Democrats had absorbed and internalized the ideal of bourgeois family life, and when faced with the resolution of this contradiction between the ideal and their program for integrating women economically and politically into society, their solution was the idealization of the woman's role in society. The tender, nurturing, child-centered mother would not be transformed; she would be transplanted from the individual family to the collective family of German society. She would fulfill her function as mother not only for her biological children but for all children.

CHANGING SOCIETY: SOCIAL DEMOCRATIC WOMEN AS SOCIAL REFORMERS

On the whole, Social Democrats held enlightened and progressive views on sexuality and its consequences. They had adopted the bourgeois ideal of the nurturing mother, but they did not deny her sexuality. They educated working-class women on different methods of birth control and fought reactionary forces that wanted to deny women information and access to birth control. They worked for changes in laws that discriminated against women in their biological and sexual capacity. They worked for reform in the areas of abortion, marriage and divorce, illegitimacy, prostitution, and protection of women as mothers (*Mutterschutz*).

Abortion

The infamous paragraph 218 of the German civil code made abortion a criminal offense punishable by a fine and jail sentence for both the woman and the doctor performing the abortion.

From the time of the national assembly, the SPD introduced resolutions in every Reichstag to change paragraph 218 so that abortion would no longer be a criminal offense. Finally, in 1925, the SPD's abortion resolution was put on the Reichstag's agenda. It was to make abortion legal if it were performed by a licensed physician within the first trimester of pregnancy.

Although the party's abortion reform, as written, did not pass the Reichstag in its original form, reform came about as a result of SPD efforts. The new law made abortion a misdemeanor rather than a felony and in effect meant that, while abortion remained illegal, its punishment was greatly minimized. Though Social Democratic women were not content with this, they considered it some progress.[23]

Typically, the abortion issue was split not along male/female lines in the Reichstag but rather along party lines. Social Democratic men and women saw abortion as a class issue, not a feminist issue. Abortion, the SPD insisted, was primarily a problem for working-class women. Bourgeois women had access to doctors who, for the right price, would take the risk of performing criminal abortions. Poor working-class women, on the other hand, had to seek out the backroom abortionist and suffer all of the consequences of illegal abortion in terms of poor health and even death. Beyond harming the health of the working-class woman, the SPD argued, illegal abortion harmed the health of the whole society in terms of the children born to women who were ill and weak from repeated pregnancies.[24]

Abortion was not an individual problem but a social problem, the SPD claimed. Most abortions occurred because of social or economic circumstances, it was argued, and society had to assume the responsibility and burden of correcting those problems, not punish poor women for seeking the only solution available to them. Women did not seek abortions for capricious reasons or because they did not want to fulfill their responsibilities and duties as mothers. They sought abortions as a result of the social and economic conditions created by capitalist society. *Genossin* editorialized: "The longing for motherhood is deeply ingrained in every healthy woman. How much longer must we tolerate that women who, for weighty reasons, abdicate the fulfillment of their yearnings must, on top of all that, appear for judgment before the courts."[25]

Social Democratic women were able to use the abortion issue to point out the contradictions of capitalism and the hypocrisy of bourgeois society. In response to those who were against abortion on religious or ethical grounds, Social Democratic women responded with a Marxist analysis. The antiabortion laws, they wrote, were formulated at a time when Prussia was seeking to expand as a military and world power. Abortion became illegal only to ensure the growth of the Prussian military and the success of imperialist adventures. The respect for human life preached by the antiabortionists was little more than sheer selfish class interest. Human life was precious or cheap as it served the interests of the ruling class and not for abstract ethical reasons. The state was guilty of hypocrisy in punishing some women for abortions while permitting others to work in health-endangering industries that resulted in a high percentage of miscarriages. Furthermore, while the state showed such high regard for the unborn life, it permitted millions of infants to die in the first year of life, most of whom could be saved if the material conditions of life were better.[26]

The basis for the socialist arguments for legal abortion was hammered out at the 1925 women's conference and stated:

> If the woman does not fulfill her social duties, society can only punish her if it gives her the prerequisites for the fulfillment of those duties. Under this basic premise, all punishable offenses which deal with the question of a woman's right to her own body and soul are to be viewed.[27]

Notwithstanding the statement regarding a woman's right to her own body and soul, Social Democratic women never used the modern feminist rationale of a woman's right to control her own body but rather always argued that capitalist society made abortion necessary because it did not provide the social and economic conditions that would make motherhood, especially multiple motherhood, possible. The implication was always that all women would love to be mothers if they could only afford it.

Marriage and Divorce Reform

Despite the 1919 Weimar constitution, which declared the
equality of the sexes within marriage, the civil law caused marriage in the Weimar Republic to remain an unequal contract
that favored the husband over the wife.

Social Democratic women had a concept of marriage as a
partnership of equals. They hoped to move from the patriarchal,
authoritarian marriage to a democratic marriage of two life com-
panions. Instead of the terms "husband" and "wife," they preferred to use the term "life companion" (*Lebensgenosse*). Social
Democratic women were not trapped in the notion of the duti-
ful wife, as they were in the ideology of the devoted mother.
Their concept of marriage and women's role within it followed
Bebel's description of women in the future socialist society. For
the socialist woman, marriage would still be monogamous, but
easily dissolved if necessary. The ideal, however, was obviously
the lifelong monogamous marriage of two devoted partners.
Marriage, they believed, was a private concern sustained by
mutual affection and, as such, based on affection rather than
property. Some of the worst abuses of bourgeois marriage
would automatically be eliminated, but "if incompatibility,
disenchantment, or repulsion set in between two persons that
have come together, morality commands that the unnatural,
and therefore immoral, bond be dissolved."[28]

Social Democratic women promoted the easy dissolution
of marriage and an equalization of the power relationship in
the family, which was sustained by the old civil code despite
the democratic concept of the family as expressed in the Weimar constitution. Daily relationships in Weimar society were
governed not by the constitution but by the civil code (*Bürger-
liches Gesetzbuch*, or BGB), and the code continued to assert
the power of the father/husband within the family. All attempts
by the SPD to change the civil code and to equalize the marital
relationship met with failure. The provisions that Social Democratic women argued against and hoped to change dealt with
control of property in marriage, authority over children, life-
style, divorce, and sexual relations. In all of these areas, the
civil code was contradictory to the socialist idea of the equal,

democratic, companionate marriage. In all of these areas, some Social Democratic women exhibited a high degree of feminist consciousness. As a high percentage of the leaders of the SPD women's movement were divorced, personal experience must have supplemented socialist analysis to move them to work for marriage and divorce reform. Regarding paragraph 1353, which obligated marital partners to sexual intercourse, Tony Pfuelf wrote that control over one's body was basic to women's equality: "If the woman is subservient in sexual relations, she will not be emancipated in the other relations of marital life."[29]

Gleichheit and *Genossin* carried articles objecting to the wife's having to assume the husband's name (paragraph 1355) and the husband's determining the residence and life-style of the couple. Ella Borman wrote in *Gleichheit:* "If the wife in individual cases has a different place of residence from the husband, there is no reason for the law to determine her place of residence. . . ."[30] *Gleichheit* also suggested that the traditional practice of the woman giving up her name upon marriage was inappropriate for the new democratic marriage. Instead, it was suggested, the new family name ought to be a double name, which would be assumed by the children until they married, in which case the sons would carry on the father's name and the daughters the mother's name.[31]

Social Democratic women also protested the economic control of the husband over the wife. A husband could forbid his wife to work, according to the civil code (paragraph 1358), and whatever financial resources a woman brought into the marriage or earned were under the control of the husband for the duration of the marriage (paragraph 1363). Marriage made a woman dependent upon a man. She gave up her property and economic independence and in addition was obligated to be sexually available—not a very equitable, democratic arrangement, Social Democratic women pointed out.

They also protested the father's authority over the children (paragraph 1627) and asked for a more equal arrangement. In place of divorce laws that made divorce difficult and contingent upon proving the guilt of one partner, SPD women favored easy divorce based on irreconcilable differences, in which dissolution of the marriage would follow the request of either partner.[32]

SPD women recognized, of course, that divorce left women
in a worse situation than men because of women's economic
dependence. They recognized that this dependence was based
on women's biological capacity to bear children. In a patriarchal,
capitalist society, it was the women's childbearing capacity that
ultimately put them in such a dependent position. A socialist
society would recognize that childbearing and child rearing were
socially indispensable functions for which women would be compensated. To free women from their dependence on men, society
had to assume the major burden for children.[33]

Though Social Democratic women were unable to bring about
the changes to provide a legal basis for democratic marriage,
their discussions of these issues were a contribution toward under-
mining the authoritarian, patriarchal German family. Of course,
questioning the authority of the father/husband was an expression of the changing material conditions that had already undermined that authority and were primary in contributing to its
further breakdown.

Social Democratic women presented a progressive alternative
not only in the areas of marriage and divorce but also in other
areas of sexuality, such as illegitimacy and prostitution. Although
a high illegitimacy rate was not a new problem in Germany, the
rate increased in the 1920s to a high of 12.6 percent in 1926.[34]
The economic and social disadvantages suffered by illegitimate
children had been a concern of Social Democrats at the national
assembly in 1919 and continued to be one of their concerns in
the 1920s. They focused primarily on the social stigma attached
to illegitimacy and worked toward forcing more support from
the biological father. Even if the enlightened attitude of the SPD
did not bring much concrete relief for the unwed mother and
her child on the national level, in Saxony the party was successful in having the state sponsor homes for unwed mothers.[35]

In the areas of prostitution and venereal disease, Social Democratic women were also proposing enlightened reform. As early
as 1919, they called for the legalization of prostitution and for
the medical control of prostitutes and their customers.[36]

By far the most intense campaign of SPD women concerned
the area of social protection for mothers (*Mutterschutz*), an area
in which the radical bourgeois feminists had been active since the

turn of the century through the League for the Protection of Motherhood and Sexual Reform (*Bund für Mutterschutz and Sexualreform*), founded in 1904.[37] Though radical bourgeois feminists were close to socialist women in their position on protection of motherhood, no bourgeois political parties shared the vision of the SPD or the radical feminists that motherhood be recognized as socially productive labor for which women should be compensated and that children had the right to receive the protection of the community.[38]

Since its beginning, the SPD had distinguished itself by struggling for protection for children and for pregnant women who worked in factories. This often expressed itself in a reactionary way by keeping women out of competition with men for jobs and helped to perpetuate the division of labor detrimental to women. The realities of the SPD's female constituency, however, did not allow the party to take any other kind of position. Women who worked in factories needed special protection in their capacity as mothers. Marie Juchacz recognized the discriminatory effect of special protection but insisted, "Social development shows clearly that we are better off struggling for the economic independence of women with special protection for women and especially for pregnant women than without it."[39]

By the 1920s, mothers were entitled to six weeks' leave before and after childbirth with partial compensation. During the 1920s, the SPD Reichstag delegation—men and women—worked to extend the six weeks following childbirth to eight weeks and to increase the compensation. They also hoped to extend protection for women from industrial workers to include women servants and farm workers. By 1929, thanks to the efforts of the SPD, the compensation for mothers was raised from 50 percent to 75 percent of their normal pay. As women were paid at a much lower rate than men, employers, of course, still did not suffer from employing women.

In conclusion, when women became active in public life, they became active in those areas and fought for those reforms closest to their traditional role. Although this perpetuated traditional attitudes and roles for women and consequently was not as desirable as women becoming engaged in all aspects of public life, it was progressive, particularly where it addressed issues of women's sexuality and procreative function.

NOTES

1. *Gleichheit* (September 4, 1914), p. 375; Luise Zietz, *Die Sozial-demokratischen Frauen und der Krieg* (Stuttgart, 1915).

2. Marie Juchacz noted that the *Arbeiterwohlfahrt* was received with great skepticism in party circles. Juchacz continually felt the need to justify the *Arbeiterwohlfahrt* on political grounds, which indicated also that she received some criticism, although there is not much public criticism. Other defenders, like Anna Blos, also felt the need to justify the existence of the *Arbeiterwohlfahrt*. See Marie Juchacz and Johanna Heymann, *Die Arbeiter-wohlfahrt* (Berlin, 1924), p. 29, and Anna Blos, *Die Frauenfrage im Lichte des Sozialismus* (Dresden, 1930), p. 133.

3. Juchacz, *Die Arbeiterwohlfahrt*, p. 30.

4. Fritzmichael Roehl, *Marie Juchacz und die Arbeiterwohlfahrt* (Hannover, 1961), p. 67.

5. Juchacz, *Die Arbeiterwohlfahrt*, p. 13.

6. Marie Juchacz, "Die Frau als Staatsbürgerin," *Frauenstimmen aus der Nationalversammlung* (Berlin, 1920), p. 15.

7. Juchacz, *Die Arbeiterwohlfahrt*, p. 15.

8. *Jahrbuch* (1929), p. 195.

9. Juchacz, *Die Arbeiterwohlfahrt*, p. 233.

10. The trend was already to be seen in 1917, when a delegate proclaimed: "Social politics on all sides, but especially social politics for women and by women." *Protokoll* (1917), p. 441. Applause was noted in the text.

11. *Protokoll* (1921), p. 11, Frauenkonferenz.

12. Ibid.

13. Ibid., p. 14.

14. Ibid., Anträge.

15. Ibid., p. 40.

16. Marie Juchacz, *Sie lebten für eine bessere Welt* (Berlin, 1955), p. 8.

17. Paul Loebe, *Erinnerungen eines Reichstagspräsidenten* (Berlin, 1949), p. 52.

18. Hans Speier, "Verbürgerlichung des Proletariats," *Magazin der Wirtschaft* 7 (1931): 595, quoted in Richard Hunt, *German Social Democracy, 1918-1933* (Chicago, 1970), p. 143.

19. Henrik de Man, "Verbürgerlichung des Proletariats?" *Neue Blätter für den Sozialismus* 1 (1930): 106, quoted in Hunt, *German Social Democracy*, p. 146.

20. Henrik de Man, *The Psychology of Socialism*, trans. Eden and Dedar Paul (London, 1927), p. 257, quoted in Hunt, *German Social Democracy*, p. 146.

21. *Genossin* (June, 1930), p. 251.

22. Regine Deutsch, *Die Politische Tat der Frau aus der Nationalversammlung* (Gotha, 1920), p. 41. Emphasis in the original. For a discussion of changing family life and concepts of childhood, see Philippe Aries, *Centuries of Childhood* (New York, 1962); Ann Oakley, *Woman's Work* (New York, 1976), pp. 10-59; Joan W. Scott and Louise A. Tilly, "Woman's Work and the Family in Nineteenth Century Europe," in *The Family in History*, ed. Charles Rosenberg (University of Pennsylvania Press, 1975).

23. *Genossin* (1926), p. 163.

24. Ibid., p. 36.

25. Ibid., p. 41. The rationales for legalized abortion are another example of the Social Democratic idealization of motherhood.

26. Ibid., p. 39.

27. *Protokoll* (1925), Frauenkonferenz.

28. August Bebel, *Woman under Socialism* (New York, 1971), pp. 343-344.

29. Tony Pfuelf, "Die Politischmündige Frau und das gesetzliche Eherecht," *Genossin* (1926), p. 293.

30. Ella Borman, "Die Gleichstellung der Geschlechter im deutschen Eherecht," *Gleichheit* (June 15, 1922), p. 109.

31. Ibid., p. 110.

32. *Genossin* (1926), p. 295. In 1925, the SPD proposed divorce reform based on irreconcilable differences.

33. *Gleichheit* (June 15, 1922), p. 113.

34. As early as 1851 through 1860, the average yearly rate of illegitimate children was 11.5 percent. See *Statisches Jahrbuch* (1933), p. 27.

35. *Genossin* (1927), p. 201.

36. *Protokoll* (1919), p. 20.

37. See Richard Evans, *The Feminist Movement in Germany, 1894-1933* (London, 1976), pp. 120-139.

38. *Frauenwelt* (1925), pp. 8-9.

39. *Genossin* (August, 1925), p. 336.

5

WOMEN AS WORKERS: REALITY AND IDEOLOGY

THE IDEOLOGY OF the SPD was rooted in reactions to the economic changes accompanying the rise of industrial capitalism. The very existence of the party was based on the emergence of an industrial working class, free from all feudal ties and obligations, which earned its living through the free sale of its labor. Similarly, the Social Democratic Women's Movement was organized around the fact that women also made up a large percentage of the industrial labor force and that there was a significant difference between working men and women. According to socialist theorists from Engels to Bebel and Zetkin, the entrance of women into the industrial labor force had great revolutionary potential. With the advent of industrialism and the change from private production in the home to social production in the factory, the objective economic conditions for the liberation of women had come into existence for the first time in history. The industrial working woman, with the heightened consciousness produced by her working conditions, was to lead the way toward the emancipation of her sex, just as, according to Marxist theory, the industrial proletariat was the class that was to lead the way toward the liberation of humanity as a whole.

The participation of women in socially productive labor, however, raised a whole set of problems, both practical and theoretical, which the socialist theoreticians had not addressed but which a political party could not avoid. In the 1920s, the SPD and the women's movement had to confront these problems again and again.

Some of these problems, such as how the procreative and socially productive functions of women were to be reconciled and what the role and place of women in male-dominated political society were to be, have already been discussed. In addition, a central issue for the women's movement centered around women's economic function at work and as a wage worker. The industrial working woman was the natural, if not the only, constituency of the woman's movement; hence, the ideology and practice of the SPD focused around her concerns. These concerns included the difficulty of organizing women into trade unions, the continued difference in the rates of pay of male and female workers, and, most significantly in the crisis of unemployment following the war and again in the Great Depression, the question of whether, at a time when jobs were scarce, women had a right to work at all.

THE HISTORICAL BACKGROUND OF WOMEN WORKERS IN GERMANY

To understand the social and economic conditions within which the women's movement functioned, it is necessary to summarize the impact of industrialization on the German working woman, with an emphasis on the changes that occurred as a result of World War I. As the industrial revolution took off in Germany, as many women as men were employed in the new factories. This was due to the fact that one of the first industries to mechanize was the textile industry, which as a cottage industry had traditionally employed many women. However, by the second half of the century, the emphasis shifted from textiles to heavy industries of steel and chemicals, and the number of women workers began to decline in relation to men. The absolute number of women working for wages, however, increased steadily between 1880 and 1925 from just under 5 million, or 24.4 percent of the female population, in 1882, to over 11 million, or 35.6 percent of the female population, by 1925.[1]

   Prior to World War I, this increase in women wage earners
was no threat to men, although in the early stages of the labor
movement it was perceived as such. The great majority of wom-
en (43.3 percent) worked in agriculture, at jobs not desired by
men.[2] As for those women who worked in industry, 90 percent
were concentrated in the "female industries" of textiles, clothing
manufacture, and confections. Those few women who worked in
"male industries" were almost all unskilled and worked at the
lowest-level jobs.[3] The fear that women would become an economic threat to men, a fear that had expressed itself in trade
union and SPD debates in the 1860s, did not materialize in Germany prior to World War I. An expanding economy and the channeling of women into certain limited sectors of the economy had
kept competition between men and women for jobs at a mini-
mum. Consequently, before the war, the question of women's
right to work was not discussed in the SPD or challenged in the
rest of German society. Only when women began entering "male
industries" during the war and economic conditions worsened
was women's right to work again questioned, not only by conservative forces but from within the working-class movement
itself.[4]
   By 1914, the tradition of a sexual division of labor into work
suitable for men and work suitable for women was well established in Germany. This division of labor was never questioned
by the SPD or the women's movement, as it was by bourgeois
feminists. Furthermore, the SPD's view that women had to be
protected from certain kinds of difficult and dangerous work
contributed to the perpetuation of the sexual division of labor.
The unfortunate consequence of a clear division of labor between men and women facilitated the practice of paying wom-
en half as much as men. While the statistics for the nineteenth
century are not completely reliable, some studies suggest that
the difference in the rates of pay between men and women
widened in the course of the century as the division between
men's work and women's work became well established. Where-
as in the 1860s women earned in some instances 70 percent of
men's wages, by 1890 they were earning on the average only
50 percent of what men earned.[5]

WORLD WAR I

World War I brought dramatic changes to women's work. Not only did the number of women who worked for wages increase, but the type of work that women did also changed greatly. As key industries lost male workers to the armed services, women were recruited to fill their places. Prior to 1914 the employment of women in heavy industry was rare, but between 1914 and 1918 there was hardly any industry in Germany that did not employ women.[6]

In the course of the war, the number of women who worked for wages increased by 130.3 percent.[7] As the total number of male workers declined and the number of women increased, by 1916 there were as many women working in German industry as men.[8] Even more significant, however, was the fact that women found entrance into a whole new range of industries. As the arms industry grew and the textile, clothing, and confectionery industries declined, women found jobs in the formerly exclusively male electrical, chemical, and machine industries. The Krupp industries, for example, which had not employed a single woman before the war, employed 11,000 women by the end of 1914. There was no hesitation in employing women for even the most physically demanding labor,[9] and to make this possible, all protective legislation affecting women workers was withdrawn as soon as war broke out. The old arguments about protecting women's health were discarded when women's labor was needed to meet the needs of the war industry.

The entrance of women into formerly exclusively male industries was met with some concern by men, who recognized the inherent threat in eliminating the traditional division of labor. It became obvious that in the future women would provide threatening competition for men, especially since they continued to work for lower wages.[10] Women moved into men's jobs, but, of course, they did not receive men's wages. Although in the course of the war the gap in wages was narrowed, women continued to work for considerably less.[11]

Another impact of the war on women was a sharp increase in female trade union membership. Between 1913 and 1918, the number of women organized in the free trade unions increased

60 percent. At first, women showed little interest in trade
unions. Those who entered the labor market considered their
work to be for the duration of the war only; and as the labor
market was relatively good, they saw no benefits to be derived
from joining unions. However, as inflation cut into their wages
and a struggle over wages developed, the benefits of trade union-
ism became increasingly clear. The trade unions also became
more aggressive during the war in demanding equal wages for
women. Although this was designed more for the protection of
men than for the benefit of women, women could only feel
that the trade unions were representing their interests more
aggressively than ever before. Unions also became more attractive
to women, as many employers showed a lack of understanding
of the situation of women, many of whom were supporting
families from their wages while their husbands were in uniform.
Thus the Dresden Bank, when confronted with the demand to
raise wages, suggested in 1918 that married men receive a 25
percent increase, single men a 15 percent increase, and women
no increase at all.[12]

Overall, through the deprivation created by the war and by
women's struggle to survive, their consciousness was raised. As
they worked at male jobs, they lost some of their traditional
feeling of inferiority and took more interest in public issues.
Women, for example, played a significant role in the expression
of mass discontent during the war. The hunger riots of the
winter of 1916-1917 were staged primarily by women,[13] as
were the first demonstrations against the war and the inflation
that came in 1915.[14]

THE END OF WAR

In 1918, 8 million soldiers returned to civilian life looking for
jobs, and while the great majority found work, a great number
did not. By February, 1919, there were still 1.1 million unemployed.[15] To ease the situation, women were encouraged to give
up their jobs to the returning veterans. Many women, no doubt,
did so gladly, content to return to home and family and to allow
a husband to support them. This, however, was not enough to

solve the unemployment problem and restore the prewar equilibrium. Consequently, demobilization orders were issued by the Ministry of War, providing guidelines for employers to ease the unemployment of veterans. These demobilization orders were comprehensive, assuring not only full employment for veterans but also a reestablishment of the prewar sexual division of labor.

The demobilization orders specified that women who could be supported by men were to be channeled into their earlier occupations, where there was a labor shortage and where they would not be "competition for men."[16] The wording of the demobilization orders is revealing of what the authorities had in mind.

> As a result of the radical change which has occurred in women's industrial work in Germany during the war, the question of the transition from a war to a peace economy is of great significance for the economy and the strength of the nation [*Volkskraft*]. It is necessary to re-integrate the labor of women into the traditional areas, be that the family, which must be encouraged but which as a result of war casualties will be possible for a reduced number of women, or be it through transference to jobs which women held before the war, or those which in the course of economic development have proven themselves suitable for women.[17]

The demobilization stressed in several instances the benefits of a return to the traditional division of labor to industry and the economy in general. Apparently it was necessary to persuade employers that retaining women at lower wages was not to their advantage. The orders also cautioned that the firing of women should be gradual, to avoid the possibility of protest and perhaps even rioting by those affected.

Despite the demobilization guidelines, unemployment did not decrease in Germany but continued to rise after March, 1919.[18] However, the unemployed were now mostly women, as employers did their patriotic duty and followed the demobilization orders, some with an enthusiasm often going far beyond the original intent. Many women who had been employed long before

the war broke out were summarily dismissed in 1919.[19] Some
firms, in addition to discharging all married women, fired unmarried mothers, with the cynical explanation that they should
have been married.[20]

The SPD and the trade unions and many women within these
organizations accepted the premise that women had to make
way for the returning veterans. While they weakly protested
the overzealous implementation of the orders, they were not,
at that point, prepared to defend the right of women to work,
nor did they draw upon the socialist analysis that only employed
women would have the consciousness and desire to struggle for
a socialist Germany.[21]

Where the sentiments of the majority Social Democrats lay
was evident even before the war. At the 1917 party congress,
opposition to working women was expressed, and the question
of applying legal restrictions to female employment was raised.
One delegate, with the support of others, noted that it would
be difficult to restrict women's work, because the possibilities
of marriage had decreased as a result of the casualties of war.
Nevertheless, many agreed that some restrictions needed to be
imposed. Another delegate alleged that the high infant mortality
rate, which between 1916 and 1917 had risen in one large German city from 14.9 percent to 31.2 percent, was reason enough
to restrict female employment, even if general unemployment
were not.[22]

Social Democratic women expressed their concern for the
returning veterans but also tried to defend women's right to
work. They emphasized the political advantages of the greater
number of working women and their heightened class consciousness. Anna Blos pointed out that women would not return to
the home after the war and that the party should make note of
this and use it to its political advantage.[23] The party, however,
did not perceive the unemployment of veterans as being to its
advantage. The demobilization orders were implemented when
the SPD was the largest and strongest political power in Germany. Consequently, it must be assumed that it concurred with
their premise. Despite weak protests over the too-zealous application of the orders, there was no respite in the firing of wom-
en workers.

The trade unions also weakly protested the indiscriminate mass firing of women. The demobilization plan itself, however, met with their approval. In fact, the trade unions met with the Ministry of War to draw up the plans and reported at the trade union congress of 1919 that their most important demands had been met in the demobilization plan.[24]

After the war, the unions were charged by the press and leftist parties (USPD and KPD) with responsibility for the demobilization. The unions in turn defended the orders as the only way to relieve unemployment. What they meant, of course, was male unemployment. They argued their rationale that each case was to be considered individually, but admitted that in practice it often happened quite differently.[25]

The trade unions' defense—that the implementation of the demobilization orders differed from their intent—does not hold up when the orders themselves are examined. It is most obvious that the orders intended nothing less than a restoration of the prewar status quo of German labor and that the trade unions and the SPD were essentially in agreement with this position.

The actions and inactions of the SPD and the trade unions following World War I show that a male-dominated political party and male-dominated trade unions cannot defend the interests of women when and where those interests come into conflict with the interests of men. Bebel's admonition that "women should expect as little help from men [in their liberation] as working men from the capitalist class"[26] was surely borne out in this instance. This first great clash of interests in the new democratic republic between men and women in the labor movement also shows the myth of the working-class solidarity of men and women that Zetkin had tried to forge. Although there was conflict between different social classes, it was never more clear that there was also conflict between men and women within each class.

The history of German feminism shows few instances of solidarity between women of different social classes, but the demobilization orders provided one such instance and drew women of all social classes together for a united effort, if only briefly. All women in the national assembly, regardless of political persuasion, protested the demobilization orders.[27]

There was also a socialist analysis of the impact of the demobilization on women. Although it was generally ignored,
it is of interest as part of the socialist ideology of women's
liberation. The analysis came from Mathilde Wurm of the
Independent Social Democrats (USPD). Generally more progressive than the SPD on all issues, the USPD was very critical
of the demobilization orders. This should not suggest, however, that in practice the USPD did more for women than the
SPD. Robert Wheeler concluded from his study of the USPD
that there was a general indifference to women and the woman question within that party.[28]

Mathilde Wurm warned of the consequence for social progress
if women were forced back into the home and traditional wom-
en's work. In keeping the labor force divided, she pointed out,
the weaker segment (women) became exploitable. To have one
segment of the laboring class weak and exploitable worked to
the detriment of the working class as a whole.[29] The organized
male workers, perceiving themselves as relatively privileged,
would be more complacent in their jobs and less likely to
agitate for social and political change. At the same time, the
existence of a mass of underemployed, underpaid workers
served to keep the more privileged workers insecure in their
positions. The consequence would be a greater docility of the
working class as a whole. The return of women to the home
was completely reactionary, Wurm said. "Only that woman can
be won to socialism who through her occupation becomes a
full member of society."[30] Socialists could hope to revolution-
ize women and win them to the struggle only by protecting
women's right to work. Lack of work, hunger, and despair
may indeed cause women to lead spontaneous protests, but
it would not lead to their systematic resistance, which could
occur only through trade unions and political organization.[31]

Despite the protests of women and the recitation of abuses
going far beyond the intent of the policy,[32] the demobilization
orders continued to remain in effect. As late as March, 1921,
two and one-half years after the end of the war, the systematic
firing of women continued in parts of the civil service.[33]

The demobilization orders were effective in reversing most
of the gains women had made during the war. Politically, the

effect of the war on the status of women was acknowledged
with the vote and constitutional equality, but the demobilization assured women continued economic inequality. In droves,
women returned to the home, the farm, or the traditional female
job ghettos. By 1925, almost two-thirds of all women working
in industry were again found in textiles, clothing, and confections.[34]

WOMEN WORKERS IN THE
WEIMAR REPUBLIC

During the 1920s, more women than ever before were employed, and while the gap between men's wages and women's
wages narrowed and there was much public discussion of the
unprecedented number of women working for wages, Weimar
did not bring substantial changes in the economic status of
women.

Between 1907 and 1925, the total female working population
increased by nearly 3 million. During that same time period, however, the number of men working increased by 4 million.[35] Furthermore, the great majority of women continued to be employed
in agriculture, where wages were low, hours were long, and the
working conditions were not likely to lead to liberation for
women. According to 1925 statistics, nearly five million, or
43.3 percent of the female working population, continued to
work in agriculture. Almost half, or 2.3 million, of these wom-
en were married. The significance of this is that reactionary politicians in the Weimar Republic often pointed to the employment
of married women as a cause of the economic problems and
crisis of unemployment. The reality was that the majority of
employed married women worked in agriculture at the lowest-
paid and most undesirable jobs. Then, as now, of course, politicians were more interested in finding scapegoats and easy solutions for economic woes than in analyzing reality.

It was reality that the absolute number of women working
in industry increased in the industrial occupations by 1 million.
At the same time, however, the number of men working in industry increased by 2.4 million.[36] Thus the Weimar Republic

did not represent a remarkable change in employment patterns; it merely continued the trend that had begun decades before, with the industrialization of Germany.

Socialist theory predicted that modern working conditions would politicize women workers, make them aware of their own best interests, and turn them in the direction of socialism. Women, however, continued to be less interested than men in trade union activities and party politics. Partially this was due to their double burden as worker/housewife-mother, but it is also related to the nature of work as women experienced it. Most worked at unskilled jobs that they considered temporary until marriage, and others worked in small industries. Only in the textile industry were women employed in groups of fifty or more at skilled jobs that were not considered temporary, and thus only textile workers experienced the conditions Marx thought would lead the proletariat to recognition of itself, of its interests and its power.[37]

One important change for women in the Weimar Republic was the increasing number of jobs in retail sales. Retail jobs made women workers more visible than ever before and may account for some of the popular perception that women were flooding the labor market. In general, commerce and transportation were the occupational groups that increased most dramatically between 1907 and 1925, from 3.5 million to 5.25 million, or 50.8 percent. The number of women in these occupations increased by 82.3 percent.[38] Most worked in retail sales in grocery stores, clothing stores, and restaurants. As in the agricultural sector, most were family members who worked in small family establishments. They were not the type of jobs that might lead a woman toward independence, toward identifying with a larger group, be it the working class or women. They were jobs that kept women well within the bounds of the traditional family structure.

The only occupation, in addition to agriculture, that experienced a decline between 1907 and 1925 was that of domestic service. Nevertheless, 12.5 percent of all women workers continued to be engaged in this most traditional of women's work.[39]

The attacks on women workers in Weimar focused primarily on the married woman, the so-called double earner, who allegedly was depriving a man and his family of income. In reality, there were few "double earners" depriving men of jobs. Most of the jobs held by married women were the lowest-paid, most undesirable jobs, in which men had no interest. The great majority, or 2.3 million married women, were employed in agriculture; 730,000 married women were employed in industry; and 427,000 were employed in commerce and transportation—primarily in retail sales.[40] Most of the married women who worked did not do so from a desire to be independent. Then, as now, women worked because of economic necessity. Most often they were the sole support of their families or supplemented the wages of a husband or father whose income was insufficient.[41]

In their study of Weimar women, Renate Bridenthal and Claudia Koonz asked why German women voted for conservative and reactionary parties that did not support their emancipation. Why would women consistently vote against their own interests? Why would any woman vote for the woman-hating National Socialists? Bridenthal and Koonz concluded that the vote made German women a conservative force in Weimar society because the objective conditions for women's liberation were not present in Weimar. Women did not have the kinds of jobs that would make them independent of men and capable of understanding their own interests.[42]

In his study of German working women, Kuczynski also concluded that the November Revolution did not bring women economic progress.[43] Although more women than ever before worked for wages in Weimar and, through expanding retail sales, women workers were more visible than ever before, Weimar did not provide the objective economic conditions necessary for women's emancipation.

WOMEN AND WORK AND THE SPD

Committed to parliamentary democracy and evolutionary socialism, the Social Democrats had neither the power nor the will to change the objective conditions necessary for the emancipation of women. However, in their ideology and programs, they remained true to the socialist position that women's emancipation was contingent upon socially productive work and economic independence from men.

The party's advocacy of women's rights and women's right
to work was not always politically advantageous. Women's rights
were not popular themes, even among the SPD working-class
constituency, and they certainly were not advantageous as the
party tried to expand its appeal beyond the working class to
the middle class. The party was already disappointed in the women's vote. Considering the low wages and types of jobs available
to women, as well as the continuation of the traditional family
structure, the party's programmatic insistence on women's right
to work must have seemed ludicrous to many women, those who
worked for wages as well as those who did not.

The SPD had been committed to women's right to work since
the nineteenth century, but, as had been noted, not always without resistance from within party ranks. With the economic crises
and unemployment of the 1920s, this policy caused the SPD
some political difficulty and had to be vigorously defended.
While the party hedged on the demobilization in its 1921 party
program, it again committed itself to women's right to work[44]
and reiterated that commitment more strongly in its 1925 Heidelberg program, when it proclaimed "the equal right of women to remunerative work."[45] Throughout the 1920s, the SPD
women's movement defended women's right to work, even
married women's, while that right was attacked from various
sides.[46]

The trade unions, which were a powerful interest group
within the SPD, took a cautious position. They also agreed
that women had a right to work; however, during times of
great unemployment, those who were not dependent on their
wages should make room for those who were. The trade unions
argued that this was not directed against married women and
that they recognized that many worked from economic necessity.
Their position was to raise the wages of the father/husband so
that married women would not have to work.[47] Obviously, the
trade unions were not interested in the more abstract theories
and problems of women's liberation.

The most militant supporters of women's right to work within the working-class movement were the women themselves. Marie Juchacz never wavered in defending that right, even when unemployment reached crisis proportions after 1929. In her 1929 address to the party congress, she emphasized, "Decisive in the woman question was and is the economic condition of woman."[48] Persuaded by Juchacz, the party passed a resolution stating that the goal of socialism required the work of women as well as men. Though women in Germany might be politically equal, economically and socially they were not yet free. The SPD also recognized the reality that driving women out of the labor force would be impossible, since modern industrial society needed the labor of large numbers of women. Hence, they charged, the notion that women belonged in the home and ought to get out of the labor force was not related to the realities of twentieth-century life.[49]

Later, at the height of the economic crisis, the SPD staunchly resolved: "The Social Democratic Party must fight the agitation against the working woman, whether she be single or married. It is not the working woman who is at fault for the growing unemployment, but rather the capitalist system. . . . We affirm our Heidelberg program. 'Equal right of women to remunerative work.' "[50]

Another point of contention in the Weimar Republic dealt with protective legislation. Here was a major source of disagreement between socialist women and bourgeois feminists. The SPD and the women's movement consistently supported protective legislation, always insisting that certain kinds of heavy and dangerous work should not be done by women.[51] The Social Democrats' more intimate acquaintance with the nature of industrial work made them especially adamant that women be spared from health-damaging work.[52] Feminists insisted that no one—man or woman—should work at health-endangering jobs. But though the SPD agreed in principle, it was less optimistic that such jobs could be eliminated or made safe immediately. In general, Social Democrats supported the continued division of labor and never analyzed how that division of labor was a useful vehicle for discrimination. They believed that the sexual division of labor was a problem for middle-class women, who were excluded from many professions because of it, and not a problem for working-class women.

As on their position on women's right to work, the SPD supported the principle that wages of women ought to equal those of men. The party believed that equal pay was in the best interest of the working class as a whole. In reality women did not compete with men for the same jobs, but the specter of the mass reserve army of women who would work for lower wages was part of the underlying fear and antifeminist senti- ment in the working class. Little progress was made toward equalizing wages, although, compared to the prewar period, the gap narrowed. Women continued to receive only 60 per- cent to 70 percent of men's wages, even when they did exact- ly the same work.[53]

The trade unions, who were in a position to do something about wages, also agreed that women ought to receive equal pay for equal work. This was a logical position for the trade unions, who were concerned about women competing for jobs with men. The unions reasoned that if an employer had to pay a woman as much as a man, he would naturally prefer to hire the man. Consequently, the trade unions fought for equal pay for women workers.[54]

The more progressive view of equal pay for different kinds of work *of equivalent value* was not promoted by the trade unions, nor was there any analysis of this within the party or the women's movement. Within the SPD, women's lower pay was seen as a question of economics. All seemed to agree that because women were physically less able to do strenuous work and were absent from their jobs more often than men, they should be paid less. Other accepted reasons included the fact that women were less skilled, more available for work, less mobile, and therefore unable to pursue better-paying jobs.

Some social analysts, both bourgeois and socialist, perceived that there was more to the problem than economics. They wrote that women received lower wages than men because of a general cultural prejudice against women.[55] Though socialists saw the working class exploited as a whole, they also believed that the weakest segment of that class—women—was even more vulnerable to exploitation because of the low value that society, men and women, placed on women and the work they do.

While some blamed an exploitative economic system and others the cultural orientation that valued women less than men, there were voices within the working class that blamed the women themselves. Because women did not join trade unions to the same extent that men did, they were blamed for not using the one leverage they had to improve their wages and working conditions. In 1914, for example, only 9 percent of the total trade union membership was female, and though the war led to an increased organization among women, by 1923 only 21.8 percent of organized workers were women.[56]

The poor representation of women in the trade unions led to an exchange within the working class in which the trade unions were accused of not recognizing the value of organizing women and of treating women poorly when they did join trade unions.[57] Interestingly, many trade unions appeared upset by the charges that they were not enthusiastic about organizing women. Some agreed that more could be done but pleaded the point that women were especially difficult to organize. Women, the unions pointed out, did not have the same interest in a job as men. Women still tended to see remunerative work as something they had to do temporarily until they could get back to their natural condition of being supported by a man.[58] Consequently, women did not receive the kind of training men got, nor did they have the courage or will to fight for the wages they deserved.[59]

Gertrud Hannah, a leader in the trade union movement, had explained some of the difficulty of organizing women. Half of all working women were either married or under 18 years old, two groups almost impossible to organize. Women under 18 did not understand the value of organization, she explained, and married women were too burdened with home and children to attend trade union meetings. They did not even have time to reflect upon their lives and to contemplate the desirability of organizing.[60] It was a vicious cycle. Women who worked did not become more conscious and liberated; they became more burdened and more oppressed, with even less time and energy to struggle out of their wage and domestic slavery.

The special problems faced by women who leave the home to do socially productive work are complex. For all of the reasons discussed, the advent of remunerative work for women did not make women more independent, more conscious of their interests. It did not produce the new woman, as socialist theory supposed. For women, their entrance into socially productive work did not mean a new independence as much as new burdens imposed upon the traditional ones. The SPD was in tune with the modern forces that drove women out of the home and into the labor market. However, except as sponsors of legislation to ease the burden of the working-class mother, they could not conceptualize any new ways of dealing with the problem of women leaving the home. Their solutions were by and large solutions arising out of the male experience: better pay, better working conditions, more organization. There were no attacks on the traditional division of labor nor any suggestion that women's domestic burdens be assumed or shared by men. Without a more sophisticated analysis of the sources of sexual oppression, the advent of more and more women as wage laborers did not mean much progress in the liberation of women.

In conclusion, the SPD, pushed by its women members, who were particularly adamant about defending women's right to work, expressed its support for the working woman—married and single—and promoted policies of equal pay for equal work. The party, however, could not or did not want to protect women during the mass firings of the demobilization. While more women (and more men) than ever before were in the labor force in the Weimar Republic, women held the lowest-paid, least desirable jobs, in agriculture, retail sales, and unskilled industrial work. Clearly, the Weimar Republic showed that the socially productive work of women did not necessarily usher in their liberation. It was the great failure of the SPD and the women's movement that they did not address the issue of the sexual division of labor, in society or at home.

CONCLUSION

By 1919, German women had won the vote and some measure of political equality. During the next fourteen years, many wom-

en worked to make that equality meaningful and to extend it to
all areas of women's lives: social, economic, and personal. As
part of a political party theoretically committed to women's
equality, Social Democratic women played an especially significant role in this struggle. They were well organized, with
a dedicated leadership, and by 1931 had a membership of
more than 230,000. Furthermore, they were backed by a
mass political party that boasted a total membership of over
1 million and shared in the power of government three times
during the course of the Weimar Republic (1919, 1923, 1928).

Social Democratic women carried on the struggle for women's
emancipation on many fronts. As part of the SPD Reichstag
delegations, they fought for legislative reforms in the interests
of women as wives, mothers, and workers. Within their own
political party, they dealt with male prejudice and sought positions of power and influence. Through the women's journals
and personal contacts, they worked to bring about change in
women's consciousness regarding marriage and personal relationships. They also tried to help women in their daily lives
through a comprehensive working-class welfare organization,
the *Arbeiterwohlfahrt*. Finally, they continued to struggle for
women's economic independence as the basis of women's
emancipation by defending women's right to remunerative
work.

Despite all of this energy and effort and despite the fact
that women, for the first time, had access to the political process,
the Weimar Republic did not witness a great leap forward in the
liberation of women. As political candidates, women were
obliged to win the favor of male-dominated parties for a place on
party lists. In the Reichstag, they received only token representation, never comprising more than 10 percent of the total body.
As legislators, women tended to vote as party members rather
than as women on issues.

Within the SPD, their power and influence remained limited,
and they tended to be relegated to concerning themselves with
"women's issues." The division of interests and influence into
a men's sphere and a women's sphere, which characterized modern bourgeois society, found its reflection in the German Social

Democratic movement. Social Democrats, men and women,
tended to see the new social role of women as not substantially
different from the role of women in the bourgeois family. Politically integrated into Weimar society, women would continue
to be the nurturers, the tender and humane reconcilers of human differences; but instead of lavishing their loving attention
on the individual family, they would play this role for society
as a whole.

As workers, women made no real economic progress. Their
wages continued to be substantially lower than men's, they
continued to work at the most undesirable jobs, and in general
they continued to depend upon marriage to save them from
lifelong labor at a dismal job or to supplement an inadequate
income. Plagued by crises and economic instability, the Weimar Republic did not provide the economic opportunities
necessary for the liberation of women. Social Democrats theoretically defended women's right to remunerative work in the face
of reactionary attitudes but did little to provide more opportunities for women.

Within the Social Democratic Women's Movement, progress
toward emancipation was also hampered by the limitations of
the socialist theory of women's emancipation. The classic socialist theory remained the theoretical cornerstone of the women's
movement. It emphasized that women's oppression was a result
of their economic dependence and identified the plight of wom-
en with that of the working class as a whole. The stress on working-class solidarity obscured the conflict of interest between
men and women within the working class. Consequently, the
SPD as a political party or a social movement failed to confront
many important issues. Within the women's movement itself,
only a few isolated voices addressed themselves to these questions.

The SPD and the women's movement did not question the
sexual division of labor but continued to support the concept
of separate but equal spheres of work and influence. Although
they confronted the social function of motherhood and demanded
social support and compensation for women's biological burden,
they did not confront the question of men's responsibility for the
socialization of children. Motherhood continued to be promoted

as the most fulfilling and important of women's social functions. Social Democratic women continued to allow men to define the priorities of their struggle, and the number one priority for Social Democratic women was to win women for the SPD as voters and members.

NOTES

1. Anna Geyer, "Die Frau im Beruf," in Anna Blos, *Die Frauenfrage im Lichte des Sozialismus* (Dresden, 1930), p. 187.

2. Blos, *Die Frauenfrage im Lichte des Sozialismus*, p. 197.

3. Juergen Kuczynski, *Die Geschichte der Lage der Arbeiter unter dem Kapitalismus* (Berlin, 1963), 18: 107.

4. "Erwerbsarbeit und Organisation der Frau," *Sozialistische Monatshefte* 1 (1918): 483.

5. Kuczynski, *Die Geschichte der Lage der Arbeiter unter dem Kapitalismus*, p. 119. Kuczynski warns that the nineteenth-century statistics on wages are not reliable and that it is difficult to draw a general conclusion on the difference in wages between men and women. Kuczynski's conclusion is that the difference in wages did not change in the course of the century (p. 127). The statistics that Kuczynski uses as examples, however, seem to indicate the contrary (pp. 116-134).

6. Agnes Karbe, *Die Frauenlohnfrage und ihre Entwicklung in der Kriegs und Nachkriegszeit* (Rostock, 1928), p. 77.

7. Kuczynski, *Die Geschichte der Lage der Arbeiter unter dem Kapitalismus*, p. 190. These statistics come from the insurance companies. The Ministry of Industry and Commerce reported only an 80 percent increase in women workers. Kuczynski believes that the insurance company statistics are a more accurate reflection.

8. Karbe, *Die Frauenlohnfrage*, p. 77.

9. Ibid., p. 78.

10. Ibid., p. 79. The printers and locksmiths, for example, protested against women working by insisting that women go through the same apprenticeship programs as men and that they not be allowed to accept lower wages than men.

11. Kuczynski, *Die Geschichte der Lage der Arbeiter unter dem Kapitalismus*, p. 193. Women's wages as a percentage of men's wages before the war and in September, 1918, were as follows:

WOMEN'S WAGES AS A
PERCENTAGE OF MEN'S WAGES

INDUSTRY	BEFORE THE WAR	1918
Food	37%	50%
Stone and earth	37%	45%

INDUSTRY	BEFORE THE WAR	1918
Leather	55%	55%
Weaving	63%	66%
Chemical	45%	55%
Metal	37%	51%
Wood	47%	55%
Machine	42%	46%
Electric	60%	55%
Paper	55%	56%

12. Karbe, *Die Frauenlohnfrage*, p. 95.

13. Luise Dornemann, "Die proletarische Frauenbewegung während des ersten Weltkrieges und der Novemberrevolution," *Einheit* (1958), p. 1676.

14. Kuczynski, *Die Geschichte der Lage der Arbeiter unter dem Kapitalismus*, p. 199. On March 18, 1915, there was a spontaneous demonstration of about 150 women before the Reichstag. On March 28, 1915, there was another demonstration. This time, about 1,500 women participated, protesting the war and the inflation.

15. Anna Geyer, *Die Frauenerwerbsarbeit in Deutschland* (Jena, 1924), p. 17.

16. "Betrifft: Frauenarbeit in der Übergangswirtschaft" (Berlin, November 9, 1918). Official document issued by the Kriegsministerium, Kriegsamt, tgb.=nr. 40/11.18.AZs2. Quoted in *Verhandlungen der Verfassungsgebenden Deutschen Nationalversammlung, Anlagen zu den Stenographischen Berichten*, vol. 335, no. 215, p. 79.

17. Ibid., p. 76.

18. Geyer, *Die Frauenerwerbsarbeit in Deutschland*, p. 19.

19. *Sten. Berichte*, 329: 2710. Some examples cited where the demobilization orders were carried out with excessive zeal were the following: In Erfurt, industrialists were asked to fire all of their female employees and replace them with men. The difference in pay would be made up by the city. In Hannover, all city employees who had jobs previously held by soldiers were to be fired. In Darmstadt, all female workers were asked to produce proof of the necessity of working. Women who had been working ten to twelve years were fired if they had parents or relatives to support them.

20. Kuczynski, *Die Geschichte der Lage der Arbeiter unter dem Kapitalismus*, p. 218.

21. Geyer, *Die Frauenerwerbsarbeit*, pp. 18-19. Geyer writes that the firing of married women was accepted even by organized workers and that this acceptance was based on the prevailing view that a married woman belonged in the home and had no right to remunerative work. This was the prevailing attitude despite the fact that economic developments had made such views obsolete.

22. *Protokoll* (1917), p. 436. These figures, if they are correct, represent an extremely high infant mortality. If the statistics are not accurate, the point still remains that SPD delegates believed that infant mortality had risen dramatically. The most probable cause for its rise, however, was not women's employment but starvation in Germany in the winter of 1917.

23. Ibid., p. 471.

24. *Protokoll der Verhandlungen der Gewerkschaften Deutschlands* (Berlin, 1919), p. 173.

25. Ibid., p. 217.

26. August Bebel, *Woman under Socialism* (New York, 1971), p.121.

27. *Sten. Berichte,* 338: 530-531.

28. Robert Wheeler, "German Women and the Communist International: The Case of the Independent Social Democrats," *Central European History* 8 (June, 1975): 133-139.

29. *Protokoll,* USPD (1919), p. 8.

30. Ibid., p. 9.

31. Ibid.

32. *Protokoll* (1920), pp. 115-117.

33. *Sten. Berichte,* 348: 2942. Tony Pfuelf protested a new order by the Ministry of the Interior that directed the firing of women in the *Bureau und Kassendienst.*

34. Blos, *Die Frauenfrage im Lichte des Sozialismus,* p. 199.

35. Ibid., p. 187.

36. Ibid., p. 198.

37. Karbe, *Die Frauenlohnfrage,* p. 135. Even in a women's industry like textiles, all of the better-paid jobs were held by men; of 33,000 overseers in the textile industry, only 1,700 were women.

38. Blos, *Die Frauenfrage im Lichte des Sozialismus,* p. 199. Employment statistics for 1925 are as follows:

MALE AND FEMALE EMPLOYMENT
BY INDUSTRY, 1925

INDUSTRY	MALE	FEMALE	PERCENTAGE WOMEN
Clothing	720,049	870,229	54.7%
Textile	533,889	672,842	55.8%
Food	926,140	420,258	31.2%
Metal	3,026,109	385,219	11.1%
Paper	364,321	171,981	32.1%
Stone and earth	594,625	92,157	13.4%
Wood	883,429	82,676	8.6%
Chemical	274,019	78,040	22.2%
Mining	836,104	11,252	1.3%

39. Ibid., p. 203.

40. Ibid., p. 195. An overview of the percentage of the population employed in different types of jobs between 1882 and 1925 is as follows:

PERCENTAGE OF POPULATION IN
VARIOUS INDUSTRIES, 1882-1925

	1882	1895	1907	1925
Agriculture	40.0%	33.6%	27.1%	23.0%
Industry	35.0%	38.9%	40.7%	41.3%
Commerce and transportation	9.7%	11.3%	14.9%	16.9%
Administration, professions	4.3%	4.7%	4.6%	5.1%
Health	0.6%	0.8%	1.1%	1.5%
Domestic service	5.7%	4.5%	3.5%	3.1%

The percentage of women employed in those fields was as follows:

PERCENTAGE OF WOMEN IN
VARIOUS INDUSTRIES, 1882-1925

	1882	1895	1907	1925
Agriculture	44.4%	40.5%	47.0%	43.3%
Industry	20.6%	23.7%	22.5%	25.4%
Commerce and transportation	5.5%	9.0%	10.2%	13.7%
Administration, professions	1.3%	1.6%	1.7%	2.5%
Health	1.0%	1.3%	1.5%	2.6%
Domestic service	27.2%	23.9%	17.1%	12.5%

The number of married women employed in those fields in 1925 was as follows: agriculture, 2,368,000; industry, 730,000; commerce and transportation, 427,000; administration, professions, 25,000; health, 35,000; domestic service, 60,000.

41. Ibid., p. 189. A 1928 questionnaire sent out by the trade unions to 250 working married mothers asked the reasons they worked. In two-thirds of the cases, the woman was the sole breadwinner of the family. In 33 cases, it was to supplement the income of the husband. In five cases, it was to be independent of the husband.

42. Renate Bridenthal and Claudia Koonz, "Beyond Kinder, Kueche, Kirche: Weimar Women in Politics and Work," *Liberating Women's History*

(Chicago, 1976), pp. 301-329.

43. Kuczynski, *Die Geschichte der Lage der Arbeiter unter dem Kapitalismus*, p. 232.

44. *Protokoll* (1921), part 4.

45. *Protokoll* (1925).

46. Kuczynski, *Die Geschichte der Lage der Arbeiter unter dem Kapitalismus*, p. 230. Laws continued to be discriminatory and antiwoman. For example, in January, 1928, the *Landesarbeitsgericht* of Berlin ruled that the marriage of a female employee was grounds for terminating her employment. The *Reichsgericht* recognized this as grounds for firing women. In September, 1928, the *Reichsarbeitsgericht* ruled that a female employee could be fired upon marriage if the marriage disturbed the business. In 1929, there were attempts to pass a law in the Reichstag forbidding married women to hold civil service positions. The SPD took a strong stand against this attempt. See *Genossin* (June, 1931), pp. 215-216.

47. Gertrud Hannah, "Wie stehen Partei und Gewerkschaften zur Erwerbsarbeit der verheirateten Frauen," *Genossin* (June, 1931), pp. 211-214.

48. *Protokoll* (1929), p. 220.

49. Ibid., p. 268.

50. *Protokoll* (1931), p. 284.

51. Marie Juchacz and other Social Democratic women were contemptuous of the bourgeois feminist view that there were no distinctions between the work men could do and the work women could do.

52. *Gewerkschafts-Archiv* (October, 1927), p. 208. Within the textile workers' union, for example, 64 percent of all pregnancies involved problems.

53. Karbe, *Die Frauenlohnfrage*, p. 129; and Anna Geyer, "Gleichberechtigung der Frau in der Erwerbsarbeit," *Genossin* (December, 1929), p. 528. Wage differences narrowed because there were fewer women in the reserve army of unemployed; more women became skilled workers; rationalization provided more jobs for women; and more women were organized.

54. *Protokoll der Verhandlungen des 10. Kongresses der Gewerkschaften Deutschlands* (Nuernberg, June 20-July 5, 1919; Berlin, 1919), pp. 56-57.

55. Max Quarck, a frequent contributor to *Sozialistische Monatshefte*, wrote, "From the beginning, a woman's work was considered less valuable than a man's work." Max Quarck, "Die Unterentlohnung der Frauenberufsarbeit," *Sozialistische Monatshefte* (December 22, 1916), p. 98. Another scholar investigating the economic reasons for lower wages for women concluded: "And therefore the question of lower pay is not a purely economic question . . . it is more than an object of economic theory, more than speculation of social-political interest. *It is in the deepest sense a very serious cultural problem.*" Hans Sperling, *Die oekonomischen Gründe für die Minderbezahlung der weiblischen Arbeitskräfte* (Berlin, 1930), p. 149. Emphasis in the original.

56. Gertrud Hannah, "Die Arbeiterin in der Gewerkschaft," *Sozialistische Monatshefte* (1922), p. 507; *Gewerkschafts-Archiv* (1924), p. 62; Karbe, *Die Frauenlohnfrage*, p. 135.

57. Max Quarck, "Organisation und Lohnpolitik der Frauenberufsarbeit," *Sozialistische Monatshefte* (1917), pp. 24-32, 143.

58. If the trade union explanation is accurate and most women perceive that it is natural to be supported by a man and unnatural to work for wages themselves, then this is another example of the bourgeoisification of the working class. The idea that it is natural for women to be economically dependent is, after all, a new idea emerging out of industrialization and the triumph of the middle class and its values and ideology.

59. *Sozialistische Monatshefte* (1917), p. 483.

60. Gertrud Hannah, "Die Bedeutung der Frauenberufsarbeit für die Gewerkschaftsbewegung," *Sozialistische Monatshefte* (1914), p. 823.

BIBLIOGRAPHY

PRIMARY SOURCES

Archival Materials

Friedrich Ebert Stiftung. SPD Archive. Bad Godesberg, Germany. Nachlass Marie Juchacz.

D1. Korrespondenz.
D2. Chronik des Frauenlebens.
D3. Sie lebten für eine bessere Welt (manuscript of the book), Frauen Ihres Jahrhunderts (unpublished manuscript).
D4. Manuskript und Material für Biographien und andere Beiträge zur Geschichte der Frauenbewegung.

Minutes, Protocols, Yearbooks

Bericht der 3. Internationalen Frauenkonferenze der sozialistischen Arbeiterinternationale, Brussels, 1928. Zurich, 1928.
Bericht des 4. Internationalen Frauenkongresses der sozialistischen Arbeiter Internationale, Vienna, 1931. Zurich, 1932.
Die ersten deutschen Sozialistenkongresse. Frankfurt/M, 1906.
Handbuch der Sozialdemokratischen Parteitage Von 1863-1909. Edited by Wilhelm Schroeder. Munich, 1910.
Jahrbücher der deutschen Sozialdemokratie. Berlin, 1926-1931.
Protokoll der Unabhängigen Sozialdemokratischen Partei Deutschlands. Berlin, 1917-1919.

Protokoll der Verhandlungen des . . . Kongresse der Gewerk-schaften Deutschlands. Nuernberg, 1919-1932.
Protokoll des Allgemeinen Deutschen Sozialdemokratischen Arbeiterkongresses, Eisenach, 1869. Leipzig, 1869.
Protokoll über die Verhandlungen des Parteitags der Sozial-demokratischen Partei Deutschlands, with *Anhang, Bericht über die Frauenkonferenz der Sozialdemokratischen Partei Deutschlands.* Berlin, 1890-1933.
Statistische Jahrbücher des deutschen Reiches. Berlin, 1914-1933.
Stenographische Berichte über die Verhandlungen des Reichstags. Berlin, 1919-1933.
Verhandlungen der Verfassungsgebenden deutschen National-versammlung. Berlin, 1919.

Periodicals

Die Frau, 1919-1932.
Die Frauenwelt, 1924-1933.
Die Genossin: Informationsblätter der weiblichen Funktionäre der Sozialdemokratischen Partei Deutschlands, 1924-1932.
Die Gesellschaft, 1924-1933.
Die Gleichheit, 1891-1922.
Die Neue Zeit, 1893-1922.
Gewerkschafts-Archiv, 1924-1933.
Gewerkschaftliche Frauenzeitung, 1916-1933.
Sozialistische Monatshefte, 1914-1933.
Vorwärts: Zentralorgan der Sozialdemokratischen Partei Deutsch-lands, 1914-1933.

Contemporary Writings by and/or for Socialist Women

Arbeiterbewegung und Frauenemanzipation, 1889-1933. Collec-tion of articles edited by Institut für Marxistische Studien und Forschungen. Frankfurt/M, 1973.
Blos, Anna. "Und die Frauen?" *Vorwärts,* October 20, 1918.
——. *Die Frauenfrage im Lichte des Sozialismus.* Dresden, 1930.
——. *Kommunale Frauenarbeit im Kriege.* Berlin, n.d.
Braun, Adolf. *Die Arbeiterinnen und die Gewerkschaften.*
Braun, Lily. *Die Frauenfrage.* Leipzig, 1901.
——. *Die Frauen und der Krieg.* Leipzig, 1915.

———. *Frauenarbeit und Hauswirtschaft*. Berlin, 1901.

Die Frau in der Politik und im Beruf. Berlin, 1928.

Dokumente der revolutionären deutschen Arbeiterbewegung zur Frauenfrage, 1848-1974. Collection of articles edited by Joachim Mueller. Leipzig, 1975.

Frauen im Kampf um Brot und Freiheit. Berlin, 1928.

Frauenstimmen aus der Nationalversammlung. Berlin, 1920.

Fuerth, Henrietta. *Die Hausfrau*. Munich, 1914.

Hannah, Gertrud. *Die Arbeiterinnen und der Krieg*. Berlin, 1916.

———. "Women in the German Trade Union Movement." *International Labour Review* 8 (July, 1923), pp. 21-37.

Juchacz, Marie. *Sie lebten für eine bessere Welt*. Berlin, 1955.

Juchacz, Marie, and Heymann, Johanna. *Die Arbeiterwohlfahrt*. Berlin, 1924.

Klucsarits, Richard, and Kuerbisch, Friedrich G., eds. *Arbeiterinnen kämpfen um ihr Recht. Autobiographische Texte*. Wuppertal, n.d.

Popp, Adelheid. *Frauenarbeit in der kapitalistischen Gesellschaft*. Vienna, 1922.

———. *Erinnerung aus meiner Kindheit und Mädchenjahre*. Berlin, 1923.

Reichstag und Frauenrechte. Weimar, 1924.

Reitze, Johanna. *Das Recht der Frau. Die Sozialdemokratie im Kampfe um die wirtschaftliche und soziale Stellung der Frau. Referat auf dem Parteitag der SPD in Augsburg, 1922*. Berlin, 1922.

Ruehle, Otto. *Die Sozialisierung der Frau*. Dresden, 1922.

Rynek, Elfriede. "Die Frauen und der Friede." *Vorwärts*, October 26, 1918.

Sender, Toni. *Die Frauen und das Rätesystem. Rede auf der Leipziger Frauenkonferenz der USPD, Nov. 29, 1919*. Berlin, 1919.

———. *The Autobiography of a German Rebel*. New York, 1939.

Schreiber, Adele. *Revolution und Frauenrecht*. Berlin, 1918.

———. *Schütz unsere Frauen und Mütter. Vortrag auf der Frauenkonferenz in Weimar, June 16, 1919*. Berlin, 1919.

Schumacher, Henry. *Die proletarische Frau und ihre Erziehungsaufgabe*. Berlin, 1929.

Vorstand der SPD. *Die Frau in der Politik und im Beruf.* Berlin, 1928.

——. *Praktische Winke für die sozialdemokratische Frauenbewegung.* Berlin, 1919, 1921.

Wachenheim, Hedwig. *Vom Grosbürgertum zur Sozialdemokratie. Internationale Wissenschaftliche Korrespondenz zur Geschichte der Arbeiterbewegung.* Berlin, 1973.

Wurm, Mathilde. *Die Frauenerwerbsarbeit. Rede gehalten auf dem Parteitag der USPD, 1919.* Berlin, 1919.

——. *Reichstag und Frauenrecht.* Berlin, 1924.

Zepler, Wally, ed. *Sozialismus und Frauenfrage.* Berlin, 1919.

Zetkin, Clara. *Die Arbeiterinnen und Frauenfrage der Gegenwart.* Berlin, 1889.

——. *Ausgewählte Reden und Schriften.* Three volumes. Berlin, 1960.

——. *Rede gehalten auf dem USPD Parteitag am 4. März, 1919.* Berlin, 1919.

——. *Zur Theorie und Taktik der kommunistischen Bewegung.* Leipzig, 1974.

——. *Zur Geschichte der proletarischen Frauenbewegung Deutschlands.* Berlin, 1958.

Zetkin, Clara, and Hoelz, Traute. *Gemeinsame Not, Gemeinsamer Kampf.* Berlin, 1931.

Zietz, Luise. *Die Sozialdemokratischen Frauen und der Krieg.* Stuttgart, 1915.

Classic Socialist Theory on Women

Bebel, August. *Woman under Socialism.* Translated by Daniel DeLeon. Reprinted from the 1904 edition. New York, 1971.

——. *Die Frau und der Sozialismus.* Berlin, 1962.

Engels, Friedrich. *The Condition of the Working Class in England.* Moscow, 1973.

——. *The Origin of the Family, Private Property, and the State.* New York, 1971.

Marx, Karl, and Engels, Friedrich. *The Communist Manifesto.* New York, 1973.

——. *The Holy Family.* Moscow, 1973.

——. *The German Ideology.* New York, 1960.

Marx, Karl. *Capital: A Critique of Political Economy.* Translated by Samuel Moore and Edward Aveling. New York, n.d.
——. *The Economic and Philosophic Manuscripts of 1844.* New York, 1964.
Padover, Saul K., ed. *Karl Marx on Education, Women, and Children.* Karl Marx Library, vol. 6. New York, 1975.
Zetkin, Clara. *Die Arbeiterinnen und Frauenfrage der Gegenwart.* Berlin, 1889.

SECONDARY SOURCES

Histories of the SPD and the Weimar Republic

Anderson, Evelyn. *Hammer or Anvil.* London, 1945.
Berlau, Joseph. *The German Social Democratic Party, 1914-1921.* New York, 1949.
Blum, George Paul. "German Social Democracy in the Reichstag, 1890-1914." Ph.D. dissertation, University of Minnesota, 1962.
Braun-Vogelstein, Julie. *Heinrich Braun. Ein Leben für den Sozialismus.* Stuttgart, 1967.
Eberlein, Alfred. *Die Presse der Arbeiterklasse, 1830-1967.* Five volumes. Frankfurt/M, 1969.
Drahn, Ernst. *Führer durch das Schrifttum der deutschen Sozialdemokratie.* Berlin, 1919.
Gates, Robert A. "The Economic Policies of the German Free Trade Unions and the SPD, 1930-1933." Ph.D. dissertation, University of Oregon, 1970.
Gay, Peter. *The Dilemma of Democratic Socialism: Eduard Bernstein's Challenge to Marx.* New York, 1952.
Gottschalch, Wilfried; Karrenberg, Friedrich; and Stegmann, Franz Josef. *Geschichte der Sozialen Ideen in Deutschland.* Vol. 3. Deutsches Handbuch der Politik. Munich-Vienna, 1969.
Hunt, Richard. *German Social Democracy, 1918-1933.* Chicago, 1970.
Jones, Arneta Ament. "The Left Opposition in the German Social Democratic Party, 1922-1933." Ph.D. dissertation, Emory University, 1968.
Klotzbach, Kurt. *Bibliographie zur Geschichte der deutschen*

Arbeiterbewegung, 1914-1945. Archiv für Sozialgeschichte, Beiheft 2. Bonn-Bad Godesberg, 1974.

Lidtke, Vernon. *The Outlawed Party: Social Democracy in Germany.* New Jersey, 1966.

Mehring, Franz. *Geschichte der deutschen Sozialdemokratie.* Two volumes. Stuttgart, 1919.

Michels, Robert. *Political Parties.* Glencoe, Illinois, 1958.

Morrill, Dan L. "The Independent Social Democratic Party and the Internationals: An Examination of Socialist Internationalism in Germany, 1915-1923." Ph.D. dissertation, University of Pittsburgh, 1968.

Nettl, Peter. "The German Social Democratic Party, 1890-1914, as a Political Model." *Past and Present* 30: 65-95.

———. *Rosa Luxemburg.* London, 1966.

Noyes, P.H. *Organization and Revolution: Working Class Associations in the German Revolutions of 1848-1849.* New Jersey, 1966.

Prager, Eugen. *Geschichte der USPD.* Berlin, 1921.

Pothoff, Heinrich. *Die Sozialdemokratie von den Anfängen bis 1945.* Bonn-Bad Godesberg, 1975.

Reichard, Richard. *Crippled from Birth: German Social Democracy, 1844-1870.* Iowa, 1969.

Ritter, Gerhard. *Die Arbeiterbewegung im Wilhelmischen Reich.* Berlin, 1959.

Rosenberg, Arthur. *Geschichte der Weimarer Republik.* Frankfurt/M, 1975.

———. *Entstehung der Weimarer Republik.* Frankfurt/M, 1973.

Roth, Guenther. *The Social Democrats in Imperial Germany.* Totowa, New Jersey, 1963.

Russell, Bertrand. *German Social Democracy.* With an appendix, "On Social Democracy and the Woman Question in Germany," by Alys Russell. London, 1896.

Schaerf, Theodore. "The German Social Democratic Party, 1918-1933: Theory and Practice in the Transition Period." Ph.D. dissertation, New York University, 1958.

Schorske, Karl. *German Social Democracy, 1905-1917: The Development of the Great Schism.* Cambridge, Massachusetts, 1955.

Schroeder, Wilhelm. *Geschichte der sozialdemokratischen Partei-organisation in Deutschland.* Dresden, 1912.

Waldman, Eric. *The Spartacist Uprising of 1919 and the Crisis of the German Socialist Movement: A Study of the Relation of Political Theory and Party Practice.* Milwaukee, 1958.

Wheeler, Robert. "The Independent Social Democrats and the Internationals: An Examination of Socialist Internationalism in Germany, 1915-1923." Ph.D. dissertation, University of Pittsburgh, 1970.

Women and the Women's Movement in Germany

Anthony, Katherine. *Feminism in Germany and Scandinavia.* New York, 1915.

Arendsee, Martha. "Die Novemberrevolution und die Frauen." *Einheit* 3 (1948), pp. 915-923.

Aron, Steffi. "Die Sozialistische Frauenbewegung Deutschlands in ihrer historisch soziologischen Entwicklung und in ihrem Verhältnis zur bürgerlichen Frauenbewegung." Ph.D. dissertation, University of Heidelberg, 1923.

Beckmann, Emmy, and Kardel, Elizabeth, eds. *Quellen zur Geschichte der Frauenbewegung.* Frankfurt/M, 1955.

Bering, Luise. "Die Frau bei den grossen Sozialisten." Ph.D. dissertation, University of Muenster, 1926.

Beyer, Hans. *Die Frau in der politischen Entscheidung. Eine Untersuchung über das Frauenwahlrecht in Deutschland.* Stuttgart, 1933.

Brandt, Gisela; Kootz, Johanna; and Steppke, Gisela. *Zur Frauenfrage im Kapitalismus.* Frankfurt/M, 1975.

Bremme, Gabrielle. *Die Politische Rolle der Frau in Deutschland.* Goettingen, 1956.

Bridenthal, Renate. "Beyond Kinder, Küche, Kirche: Weimar Women at Work." *Central European History* 6 (June, 1973).

Bridenthal, Renate, and Koonz, Claudia. "Beyond Kinder, Küche, Kirche: Weimar Women in Politics and Work." In Berenice Carroll, ed., *Liberating Women's History.* Chicago, 1976, pp. 301-329.

——. "Something Old, Something New: Women between the Two World Wars." In Renate Bridenthal and Claudia Koonz, eds., *Becoming Visible: Women in European History*. Boston, 1977, pp. 422-444.

Deutsch, Regine. *Die Politische Tat der Frau*. Gotha, 1920.

Dornemann, Luise. "Die proletarische Frauenbewegung während des ersten Weltkrieges und der Novemberrevolution." *Einheit* 13 (1958), pp. 1670-1683.

——. *Clara Zetkin. Ein Lebensbild*. Berlin, 1957.

Evans, Richard. *The Feminist Movement in Germany, 1894-1933*. London, 1976.

Freundlisch, Emmy. *Die industrielle Arbeit der Frau im Kriege*. Vienna, 1918.

Fuelles, Mechthild. *Frauen in Partei und Parliament*. Cologne, 1969.

Geyer, Anna. *Die Frauenerwerbsarbeit in Deutschland*. Jena, 1924.

Gosche, Agnes. *Die organisierte Frauenbewegung*. Two volumes. Berlin, 1927.

Hackett, Amy. "The German Women's Movement and Suffrage, 1890-1914: A Study in National Feminism." In Robert Bezucha, ed., *Modern European Social History*. Lexington, Massachusetts, 1972, pp. 354-386.

——. "The Politics of Feminism in Wilhelmine Germany, 1890-1918." Ph.D. dissertation, Columbia University, 1976.

Honeycutt, Karen. "Clara Zetkin and the Women's Social Democratic Movement in Germany." Ph.D. dissertation, Columbia University, 1976.

——. "Clara Zetkin: A Socialist Approach to the Problem of Women's Oppression." *Feminist Studies* 3, no. 3/4 (Spring-Summer, 1976), pp. 131-144.

Karbe, Agnes. *Die Frauenlohnfrage und ihre Entwicklung in der Kriegs und Nachkriegszeit*. No. 6. Hamburger Wirtschafts und Sozialwissenschaftliche Schriften. Rostock, 1928.

Kater, Michael. "Krisis des Frauenstudiums in der Weimarer Republik." *Vierteljahrschrift für Sozial und Wirtschaftsgeschichte* 59 (1972).

Koehler-Wagnerova, Alena. *Die Frau im Sozialismus*. Hamburg, 1974.

Koonz, Claudia. "Conflicting Allegiances: Political Ideology and Women Legislators in Weimar Society." *Signs* 1 (Spring, 1976), pp. 663-683, part 1.

Kuczynski, Juergen. *Die Geschichte der Lage der Arbeiter unter dem Kapitalismus.* Vol. 18. *Studien zur Geschichte der Lage der Arbeiterin in Deutschland von 1700 bis zur Gegenwart.* Berlin, 1965.

Lichey, Margarete. "Sozialismus und Frauenarbeit: Ein Beitrag zur Entwicklung des Deutschen Sozialismus von 1869-1921." Ph.D. dissertation, University of Breslau, 1927.

Lion, Hilde. *Zur Soziologie der Frauenbewegung.* Berlin, 1926.

Mabry, Hannelore. *Unkraut ins Parlament. Die Bedeutung weiblicher parlamentarischer Arbeit für die Emanzipation der Frau.* Munich, 1971.

Mason, Tim. "Women in Germany, 1925-1940: Family, Welfare, and Work." *History Workshop: A Journal of Socialist Historians* 1: 74-113 and 2: 5-32.

Marx, Ingeborg. *Frauenarbeit in der Zeitenwende.* Essen, 1961.

Menschik, Jutta. *Gleichberechtigung oder Emanzipation.* Frankfurt/M, 1971.

Merfeld, Mechthild. *Die Emanzipation der Frau in der Sozialistischen Theorie und Praxis.* Hamburg, 1972.

Newman, Robert Paul. "Socialism, the Family, and Sexuality: The Marxist Tradition and German Social Democracy before 1914." Ph.D. dissertation, Northwestern University, 1972.

——. "The Sexual Question and Social Democracy in Imperial Germany." *Journal of Social History* 7 (1974), pp. 271-286.

Oekinghaus, Emma. *Die gesellschaftliche und rechtliche Stellung der deutschen Frau.* 1925.

Puckett, Hugh W. *Germany's Women Go Forward.* New York, 1930.

Quataert, Jean Helen. "The German Socialist Women's Movement, 1890-1918: Issues, Internal Conflicts, and Main Personages." Ph.D. dissertation, University of California at Los Angeles, 1974.

——. *Reluctant Feminists in German Social Democracy, 1885-1917.* Princeton, New Jersey, 1979.

Reicke, Ilse. *Die Frauenbewegung. Ein geschichtlicher Überblick.* Leipzig, 1929.

Roehl, Fritzmichael. *Marie Juchacz und die Arbeiterwohlfahrt.* Hannover, 1961.

Ruehle-Gerstel, Alice. *Die Frau und der Kapitalismus.* Frankfurt/M, 1972.

———. *Das Frauenproblem der Gegenwart, Eine psychologische Bilanz.* Leipzig, 1932.

Schlette, Ruth. "Neue Veröffentlichungen zur Geschichte der Frauenbewegung." *Archiv für Sozialgeschichte* (1974), pp. 631-636.

Siemsen, Anna. *Frau und Sozialismus.* Berlin, 1944.

Sperling, Hans. *Die ökonomischen Gründe für die minderbezahlung der weiblichen Arbeitskraft.* Berlin, 1930.

Strain, Jacqueline. "Feminism and Political Radicalism in the German Social Democratic Movement, 1890-1914." Ph.D. dissertation, University of California, 1964.

Strecker, Gabriele. *Hundert Jahre Frauenbewegung in Deutschland.* Wiesbaden, 1952.

Sveistrup, Hans, and Zahn-Harnack, Agnes. *Die Frauenfrage in Deutschland, 1790-1930, Strömungen und Gegeströmungen.* Vol. 1. Burg bei Magdeburg, 1934. Vol. 2. Berlin, 1964. Vol. 3. Cologne, 1961.

Thoennessen, Werner. *Frauenemanzipation. Politik und Literatur der Deutschen Sozialdemokratie.* Frankfurt/M, 1969.

Twellman, Margrit. *Die Deutsche Frauenbewegung Ihre Anfänge und Erste Entwicklung, 1843-1889.* Two volumes. Meisenheim am Glan, 1972.

Wheeler, Robert. "German Women and the Communist International: The Case of the Independent Social Democrats." *Central European History* 8 (June, 1975): 113-139.

Zahn-Harack, Agnes. *Die Frauenbewegung, Geschichte Probleme, Ziele.* Berlin, 1928.

Other Works Consulted

Aries, Philippe. *Centuries of Childhood.* New York, 1962.

Beard, Mary R. *Woman as Force in History.* New York, 1973.

De Beauvoir, Simone. *The Second Sex.* New York, 1968.

Benston, Margaret. "The Political Economy of Women's Liberation." *Monthly Review* 21 (September, 1969): 13-27.

Boxer, J. Marilyn, and Quataert, H. Jean. *Socialist Women and European Socialist Feminism in the Nineteenth and Early Twentieth Centuries.* New York, 1978.

Briffault, Robert. *The Mothers.* New York, 1927.

Childe, Gordon. *Social Evolution.* London, 1952.

Duverger, Maurice. *The Political Role of Women.* Paris, 1955.

Firestone, Shulamith. *The Dialectic of Sex.* New York, 1961.

Fromm, Erich. *The Crisis of Psychoanalysis.* New York, 1970.

Guettel, Charnie. *Marxism and Feminism.* Toronto, 1974.

Held, Virginia. "Marx, Sex, and the Transformation of Society." In Carol Gould and Marx Wartofsky, eds., *Women and Philosophy: Toward a Theory of Liberation.* New York, 1976, pp. 168-184.

Hirsch, Helmut. *August Bebel: Sein Leben in Dokumenten Reden und Schriften.* Cologne, 1968.

Janssen-Jurreit, Marie Louise. *Sexismus: Über die Abtreibung der Frauenfrage.* Vienna, 1976.

Klein, Viola. *Feminine Character: History of an Ideology.* Urbana, Illinois, 1973.

Kirkpatrick, Jeane J. *Political Women.* New York, 1974.

Koepcke, Cordula. *Die Frau und die Gesellschaft.* Munich, 1973.

Kollontai, Alexandra. *Autobiography of a Sexually Emancipated Communist Woman.* New York, 1975.

——. *Sexual Relations and the Class Struggle: Love and the New Morality.* Bristol, 1972.

Lemons, J. Stanley. *The Woman Citizen: Social Feminism in the 1920s.* Urbana, Illinois, 1975.

Lichtheim, George. *The Origins of Socialism.* London, 1969.

Manuel, Frank. *The Prophets of Paris.* New York, 1965.

Marcuse, Herbert. "Marxismus und Feminismus." *Jahrbuch Politik 6.* Berlin, 1974, pp. 49-53.

——. *Eros and Civilization.* New York, 1955.

Mitchell, Juliet. *Woman's Estate.* New York, 1973.

——. "Women: The Longest Revolution." *New Left Review* 40 (November-December, 1966): 11-37.

Oakley, Ann. *Woman's Work.* New York, 1976.

Pomeroy, Sarah P. *Goddesses, Whores, Wives, and Slaves in Classical Antiquity.* New York, 1976.

Preller, Ludwig. *Sozialpolitik in der Weimarer Republik.* Stuttgart, 1949.

Reed, Evelyn. *Woman's Evolution.* New York, 1975.

———. *Problems of Women's Liberation.* New York, 1972.

Riasanovsky, Nicholas. *The Teachings of Charles Fourier.* Berkeley, 1969.

Rowbotham, Sheila. *Women, Resistance, and Revolution: A History of Women and Revolution in the Modern World.* New York, 1972.

———. *Woman's Consciousness, Man's World.* Middlesex, England, 1973.

INDEX

About the Author

Renate Pore received her Ph.D. in history from West Virginia University in Morgantown, West Virginia. Her publications include *Toward the Second Decade: The Impact of the Women's Movement on American Institutions* (with Betty Justice, Greenwood Press, 1981).